How it Works...
How to Fix it
APPLIANCES

Rand McNally & Company

Contents

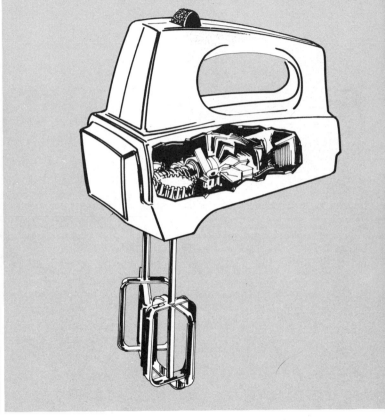

Chapter One

Getting Down
To Basics

Before you attempt to make any type of appliance repair, you should first have an understanding of how the machine operates. In the following pages, you will find specific information and repair instructions concerning each appliance, but first you must understand the basic elements common to most appliances. If you know what you are doing even before you open the case or the housing of an appliance, you can keep the job from becoming a tedious and exasperating chore.

BASIC ELECTRICAL PRINCIPLES

As you might expect, you should know something about the nature of electricity before you begin to consider the appliance itself. Electricity is the movement of electrons in a conductor. Picture a straw or tube filled with marbles. When you push a marble into one end, another marble is expelled from the opposite end; you have caused a flow of movement of the marbles within the tube. Electricity works according to similar principles.

Every material object consists of atoms which, in turn, consist of protons and electrons. The protons (the nucleus) have a positive charge, while the electrons have a negative charge. The electrons, held near the nucleus by their opposite electrical charge, whirl around the nucleus in an orbit. In some atoms, certain electrons are not bound as tightly to the nucleus as others. These "free electrons" can be moved back and forth within the conductor (wire) when a pressure, called voltage, is applied.

Materials whose atomic structures possess many free electrons make good conductors, and these are the materials that can be used for making wire — i.e. copper, aluminum, and silver. Other materials which have very few free electrons are insulators because they will not permit many electrons to pass. Plastic, rubber, and glass are commonly used insulators. There is, however, no perfect insulator; it is all a matter of degree.

The number of electrons flowing past any given point in a wire is the current, and the unit of measure for current flow is the ampere. A restriction that slows down this flow of electrons (such as a smaller diameter wire or another material which does not conduct as well spliced into the circuit) is called resistance. Resistance is measured in ohms.

These three characteristics of any electrical circuit — voltage, current, and resistance — are essential when analyzing an electrical component. A technician uses an instrument called a volt-ohmmeter, or VOM, to measure voltages and resistance. Since each one of these characteristics is directly related or directly proportional to the others, a reading or interpretation of any one of them can be a great help in problem solving. Nevertheless, for fixing most appliance problems you will not need to use a VOM.

If you find that you want to continue learning about home appliances, then you should purchase one of the less expensive volt-ohm-meters available today. For most practical purposes, however, a simple battery-powered continuity tester is sufficient. Whether you are using a battery-powered test light or the most expensive ohm-meter, the electrical principles are still the same. Since you generally use the continuity tester with the appliance completely disconnected from the voltage source, a continuity test is the safest type of test. Moreover, it is usually the best way of diagnosing appliance repair problems.

An electrical circuit forms a closed loop. Since there must be a path in and out for the current to flow, the components that you find on home appliances always have two leads. Such a closed or continuous circuit must exist within any electrical component as well as within the complete circuit itself. To test the component with a continuity tester, first unplug the appliance and then disconnect at least one of the wires from the component to prevent feedback. Clip one lead of the tester to one of the component terminals or to one of the wires leading into the component, and clip the other lead to the other terminal. The buzzer (or light) on the tester should indicate continuity if the component is good. If the buzzer sounds, then continuity exists within the component. If it does not, then the component is said to be "open."

A switch operates in the same manner. When a switch is on, it should indicate continuity. When the switch is off, it should be open (meaning that the electrical circuit is open and no electric current can flow). For a working component to be operative, it must be closed and indicate continuity. A switch, of course, can indicate either open or continuity, depending on the position of the switch at the time.

While it is important for the electrical components to indicate continuity, it is also important that the electrical current be completely insulated from the metallic part of the housing — like, for example, the appliance cabinet. Such insulation is imperative to prevent electrical shock. You can test the metallic cabinet with a continuity tester. Turn the appliance on, and check the current flow from each lead of the plug to the frame of the housing. If you find continuity, then the appliance is grounded and should be replaced. Current flowing to the frame of the machine could deliver a dangerous electrical shock to anyone who uses the appliance.

When current flows through a conductor, lines of magnetic force are set up around the conductor itself. These lines are weak until the conductor is wound into a coil, which concentrates the magnetic force in a small area and puts it to work. In appliances, an electromagnetic coil is often used to attract a spring-loaded arm (called an armature or plunger) when the current flows through the coil. This device is called a solenoid — an electromagnetic contrivance which is used to create mechanical energy or motion. Solenoids take many different forms: they may be part of a relay, which is simply a solenoid coil with a switch attached to turn itself on and off by remote control; or they may be found in the inlet valves of a washing machine where they open and close the water line in response to the machine's timer.

Another common use of this magnetic force is in an electric motor, where the coils are arranged in such a way that they cause an armature to spin and put the appliance to work. Several types of motors are used in electric appliances. The part that spins is the rotor, while the part that remains stationary is

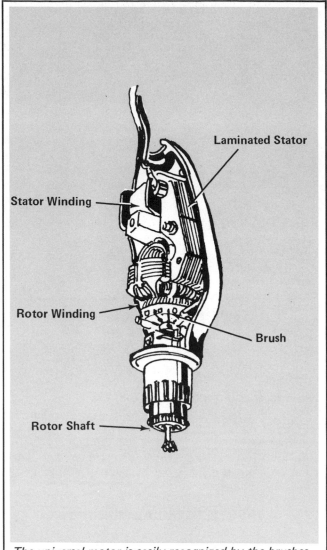

The universal motor is easily recognized by the brushes that conduct current from the field to the rotor.

called the stator. The stationary coils of wire are the fields. The rotor turns within bearings, which are located in the bell housings at the two ends of the motor. Many appliances have bearings which require no lubrication, while others have oil caps or wicks that are readily noticeable. It is important that you never over-oil the bearings. Usually, a couple of drops of oil each year are all that you need to lubricate the bearings. Frequently, the appliance manufacturer offers specific recommendations for the type of oil you should use, but if there are no such recommendations, you can generally use SAE-20 nondetergent motor oil.

TYPES OF MOTORS

The universal motor, easily recognized by the brushes that conduct current from the field to the rotor, is the only motor that you are likely to find in an appliance that has coils of wire wound in the rotor as well as in the stator. It is called a universal motor because it operates on either alternating current (AC) like that found in a home, or direct current (DC) like that which comes from a battery.

The universal motor is powerful at low speeds, and it is capable of reaching very high speeds. In most appliances and power tools in which universal motors are used, some sort of speed control is built in. Although the speed control is generally in the form of a resistor or rheostat, it can also be accomplished by shifting the position of the brushes. Sometimes, the field windings are tapped, with leads coming from various points within the coil to alter the resistance and thus to provide several specific speeds. A governor arrangement is another way to allow a full range of speed control. Finally, solid state devices are used — particularly in newer appliances — to control motor speeds as well as to allow high torque within each speed range.

Many small appliances — fans, can openers, and others where low turning force or torque is required — use shaded-pole motors. You will recognize shaded-pole motors by the heavy shading coil (a heavy conductor) which cuts across the stator laminations (the many pieces of metal that are bonded together and around which the field coils are wound).

Many battery-operated appliances, such as electric knives, utilize miniature DC motors. In such motors, the armature or rotor has windings and it also has brushes, but the field contains no coil. The motor's magnetism is obtained from permanent magnets. Though small in size, the miniature DC motors provide sufficient power to do the job for which they are designed.

Clock motors or synchronous motors are found in many appliances, from the smallest to the largest. In the small alarm clock, the motor turns the hands; on the largest refrigerator, the motor initiates the defrost cycle. They are called synchronous motors because they sense the 60-cycle per second pulses in the alternating current on the power supply line, and then use these regular pulses to provide a very constant running speed. Although synchronous motors lack power, they can be connected to a team of drive gears to turn such fairly heavy mechanisms as washer timers or defrost timers on refrigerators — or other primary mechanisms that are intended to turn very slowly.

Split-phase motors are used on some larger appliances, even though their starting torque or turning force is limited. Often found on washing machines, dryers, and dishwashers, the split-phase motor requires an auxiliary winding (called the starting winding) to start the rotor spinning. The starting winding is wound on top of the main winding or running winding of the motor, and it is positioned so that its magnetic force will cause the armature to spin when energized. When the rotor begins to approach full speed (around 1750 rpm for a common

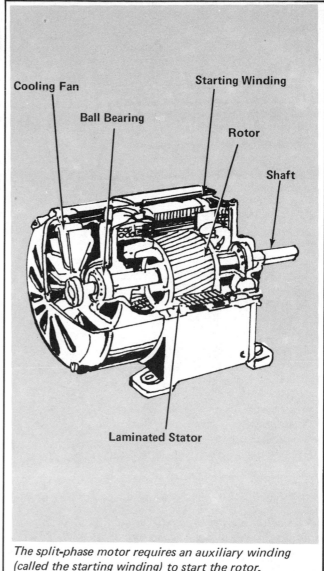

The *split-phase* motor requires an auxiliary winding (called the starting winding) to start the rotor.

split-phase motor with four running coils in its fields), excessive current begins to build up in the starting winding. Since the excessive current could damage the winding, the starting winding unit must be switched out of the circuit. It can be switched out of the circuit in one of two ways: by a mechanical switch that turns off the starting winding, or by a relay in the line to the starting winding that opens the circuit when the current gets heavy.

Capacitor motors provide higher starting torque for heavy-duty applications. Similar to split-phase motors, capacitor-run motors have a capacitor added to the running winding to increase its efficiency and running torque. A capacitor is a storehouse for electricity. Some motors, particularly those found in air-conditioning compressors, are called permanent-split-capacitor (or PSC) motors. These motors have a large oil-filled running capacitor that is

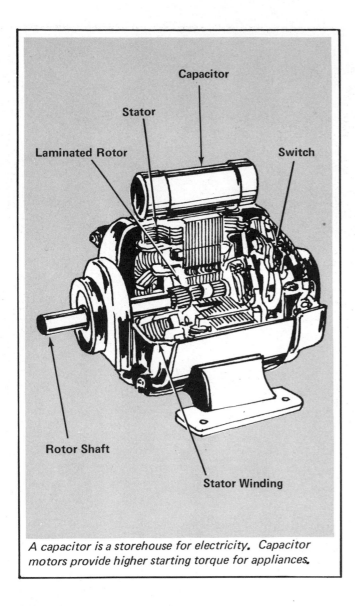

A capacitor is a storehouse for electricity. Capacitor motors provide higher starting torque for appliances.

mechanical gear train — all of which vary with the type of appliance. A switch simply closes a circuit or opens it, and you can test a switch easily. Heating elements and lights are also easy to test because they require a continuous electrical circuit to operate. Wiring, connections, and terminals should all be tight, clean, and in good contact with their mating parts. When you find it necessary to replace a terminal — particularly one that is "burned off" — be sure that it is bright and shiny when you get it all together. Otherwise, another failure will soon occur.

USING A CONTINUITY TESTER

To test a switch, touch the test leads to the prongs on the plug of an electrical appliance. Trip the appliance switch off and on. If the appliance switch is in good condition, the test buzzer or lamp should go on when you close the switch and off when you open the circuit. Thus, the continuity tester allows you to verify the condition of a switch without dismantling the appliance.

To test a thermostat, however, you must take the appliance apart. With the appliance disassembled, touch the test leads to the wires that go to the contacts on the thermostat switch. If the switch is making good contact, the tester will indicate continuity. Now, manipulate the thermostat knob or lever that changes the temperature setting until you see the switch contacts open; the tester should then stop lighting or buzzing.

When testing a heating element, touch the test leads to the end leads of the element. If the element is burned-out — that is, open-circuited so that there is no continuity through it — the tester will not light or buzz. If the element is in good condition, then the continuity tester will tell you so. If the heating element has a high resistance (a hot pad for instance), the tester light may glow only dimly. That tells you there is not much current getting through that high resistance; in other words, the element is still in good shape.

To test the brushes in a universal motor, remove the appliance cover, disconnect the motor lead wires from the remainder of the circuit, and tag the wires so that you will be able to put them back in the right place. When you touch the test leads to the motor wires, the continuity tester should light or buzz. Now, slowly revolve the motor shaft by hand. If the brushes are bad, the tester light will flicker noticeably and even go off during some part of the shaft's rotation. Good brushes making good contact should produce a steady light or sound from the continuity tester.

When testing an appliance for grounding, touch one test lead to the frame of the appliance and the other test lead to the appliance cord (run the lead end through the little holes in the plug so as to touch both at the same time). If the continuity tester lights or buzzes, then you know that the appliance frame has a fault ground and should be replaced.

in series with the starting winding. In this circuit, no starting relay or centrifugal switch is used. Instead, the capacitor causes a voltage shift as the motor approaches full speed, causing the starting winding to act as a running winding and actually increase the running efficiency of the compressor.

Motors of all types have the same basic needs. They must run cool, which means that air must circulate around and through them. Keep all motors dusted and free of lint or dirt. If the motors have oil caps on the end bells where the rotor shaft comes out of the motor housing, lubricate them according to the manufacturer's instructions — or at least once yearly. Make sure that belts attached to the motors are never too tight. Generally, a belt attached to a motor should be adjusted to have about 1/2-inch of play between the motor and the nearest pulley.

Other basic parts of home appliances include heating elements, switches, wiring, and the

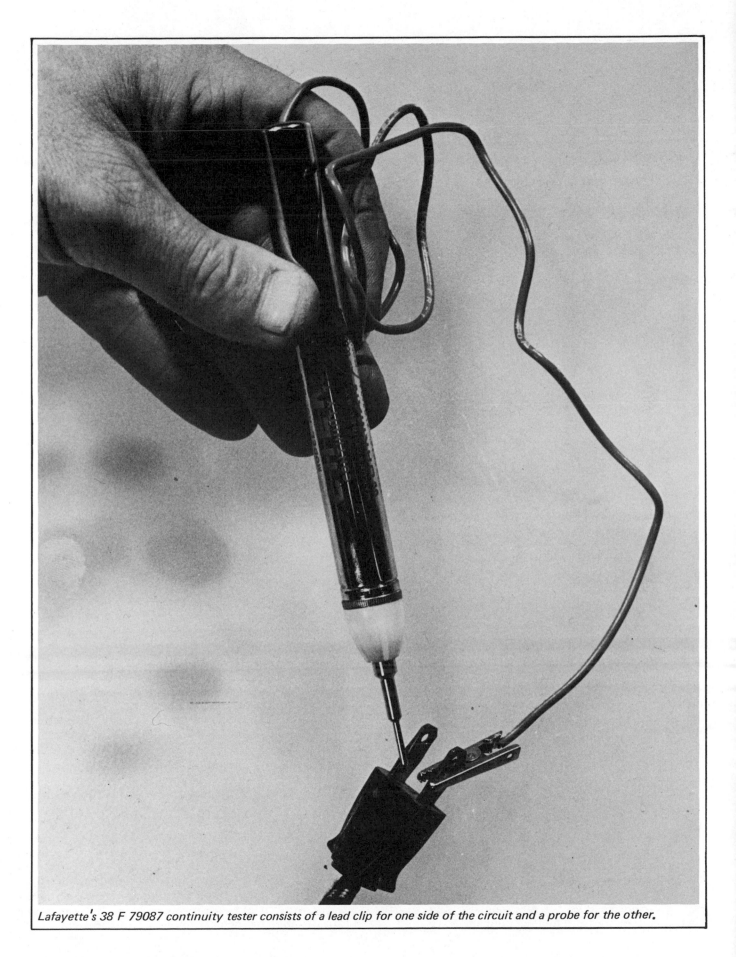

Lafayette's 38 F 79087 continuity tester consists of a lead clip for one side of the circuit and a probe for the other.

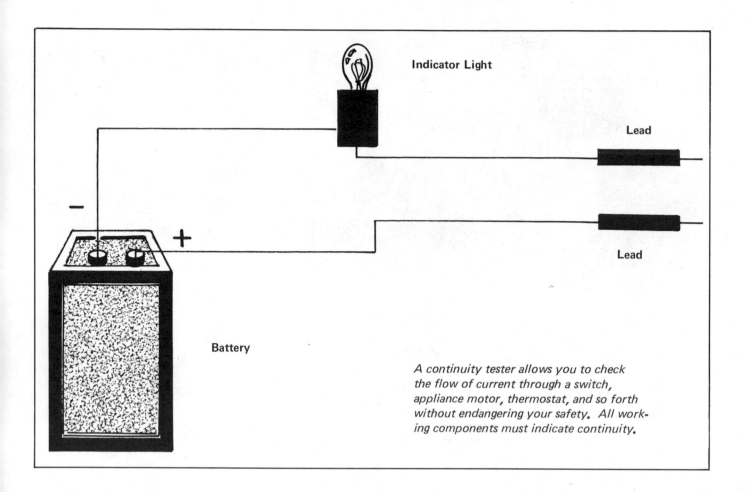

Indicator Light

Lead

Lead

Battery

A continuity tester allows you to check the flow of current through a switch, appliance motor, thermostat, and so forth without endangering your safety. All working components must indicate continuity.

You can test the safety ground (green wire in a three-wire cord) the same way. Touch one tester lead to the appliance frame, and the other to the pin on the three-wire plug. The tester should go on, thereby indicating that the safety ground wire is continuous from plug pin to appliance frame.

To test either a solenoid coil or a field coil, disassemble the appliance far enough to allow you access to the solenoid wires. Disconnect the solenoid from the remainder of the circuit, and tag the wires. Touch the test leads to the solenoid coil lead wires. If you fail to get a response from your continuity tester, the coil is open-circuited; perhaps the coil contains a broken wire. If the coil is good, the tester will indicate continuity.

On appliances where the cord is flexed constantly (like a vacuum cleaner), the cord can develop a break in one of the wires. When that happens, the appliance turns on and off erratically. To test the cord, remove it from the appliance and twist the wires together at the end of the cord. Touch a test lead to each of the plug prongs, and the tester should go on. Then, wiggle the cord at various points along its length. If at some spot the tester flickers off and on when you bend the cord in a certain way, there is a break in the wire. Discard the defective cord and replace it with a new one. Be sure to use heat-resistant cords on heating appliances.

SAFETY FIRST

Making safety your top priority is always a good policy, but it is absolutely mandatory when you start to do your own appliance repairs. The cardinal rule in servicing electrical appliances is to unplug the machine before you do anything else. Equipment that is permanently wired, such as a built-in dishwasher or a range, must be disconnected from the power lines before you begin any service procedures. Yet, even with an appliance unplugged, danger may still exist. Capacitors, like those on the compressors of air conditioners and refrigerators, can be hazardous to handle because they store electricity. Therefore, after you unplug an appliance that has a capacitor, place a 20,000 ohm, two-watt wire-wound resistor (available from a TV parts store) across the terminals of the capacitor before you touch or test it.

Once you deenergize the appliance, you can test any component or circuit with a battery-powered light or test meter. Never rush to remove the service panels; frequently, you can diagnose the repair problem with the continuity tester while all of the panels are still in place. You can also use a continuity tester to determine if a ground fault exists in the appliance. Such an appliance should be disconnected and taken out of service at once. The same is true for components; test components for

If you work with an electric drill that possesses a fault ground, you are taking a serious safety risk. Suppose you were standing on a damp concrete floor wearing old and worn work shoes. Current could go right through you to the wet floor, jolting you with a serious, perhaps fatal, shock.

ground faults and replace any hazardous parts before using the appliance.

Many appliances and portable tools are safety grounded. They have a round third prong on the plug to make a connection to the earth ground of your home's electrical system. If a ground fault occurs within a grounded appliance, current passes to the earth ground rather than through the body of the user. Never remove the extra prong on a ground plug, and be sure that the receptacles in your home are properly grounded before you use a portable tool in a dangerous location. Never take any chances with the grounding system of any electrical circuit. It takes a very small amount of current — less than that required to light the bulb of a flashlight — to be fatal in many instances.

Here is an example of what can happen when working with an unprotected ungrounded tool. Imagine that you are working in the basement, standing on a damp concrete floor, and wearing old and worn work shoes while using an electric drill. And, suppose the drill has a fault ground — say at the end of the coil. If the cord is plugged in so that the wire going to the fault ground end of the drill wiring is the grounded (white wire) end, nothing happens. The drill operates normally. If the plug were to be pulled out of the receptacle, however, rotated in a semicircle and plugged in again, the fault ground would now be connected to the black hot wire. More importantly, you would now be in touch with the hot wire through the fault ground. Current could and would go through you, through your electrically leaky shoes, and through the wet floor right into the earth. The resulting shock would cause your muscles to tighten, making you grip the drill all the tighter. It could be fatal.

Of course, the fault ground does not have to be at one end or the other of the internal circuit. A fault anywhere in the internal circuit can cause a fatal shock.

Many appliances, particularly portable tools,

are double insulated. This means that the electrical components are isolated from any current-carrying parts of the housing. Double insulation is usually accomplished with a plastic housing and with plastic parts between the electrical components and any metal components (such as the chuck on an electric drill). Never assume that such tools are foolproof, however. You still must use reasonable caution with double-insulated devices. When you drill into a wall, for instance, the bit and chuck can become "hot" if you strike a concealed wire. Double insulated appliances have no third prong on their plugs to ground them, and it takes a professional to make sure that the electrical insulation is sufficient to withstand high voltage. For this reason, most double-insulated tools must be returned to an authorized servicing agent or to the manufacturer for repairs within the housing itself.

Another way to protect yourself against electrical shock is to install a Ground-Fault Interrupter in every circuit. This device constantly monitors the leakage to ground. If it detects a dangerous level of current flowing to the ground, it turns the circuit off until you repair the ground fault and reset the interrupter. The GFI takes the place of the circuit breaker in your electrical panel, and it is required for all outdoor receptacles and bathroom circuits in new construction.

Never operate any appliance with its access panels or servicing panels removed. Keep your hands away from moving belts, gears, or any other parts of the mechanism, and watch for sharp edges around cabinet openings. When checking fuses, be sure to pull the switch to disconnect the power before attempting to remove a fuse. Stand on a dry board or other insulator when working with an electrical box, and never remove an appliance panel until all power is disconnected. By observing these few safety rules, you can assure both your own and your family's continued well-being whenever you decide to tackle appliance repair projects.

Chapter Two

Heat-Producing Appliances

Of the small appliances which use a heating element to accomplish their primary function, most have the heating element and its control system as the only electrical components. In others, such as a portable electric heater, a small motor may also be used in addition to the heating element in order to force air through the unit.

One group of these appliances — including electric skillets, frying pans, and fondue pots — has the heating element cast into the base of the unit. In all of these appliances, the heating element itself is not serviceable, although the control (a thermostat with a probe that senses the temperature in the pan) is detachable and often serviceable.

THERMOSTATS

Any switch that turns on and off in response to changes in temperature is called a thermostat. Such switches come in all shapes and sizes. There is a thermostat that controls your furnace; there is one that controls the temperature inside your refrigerator; and there is a thermostat on heating appliances. Many of these thermostats are the bimetal type, which means that the switch is actuated by two pieces of metal bonded together into a strip. Since all materials respond to temperature changes at different rates, the bimetal strip bends when heated; the two metals expand at different rates, causing a bending action. The bending can be put to good use in turning a switch on and off, thereby controlling temperatures at very precise levels.

Bimetal switches come in many different sizes and shapes to suit different purposes. Sometimes, the strip may be several inches long with a contact mounted on each end. If one of the contacts is movable, the thermostat is adjustable. Thermostats which cannot be adjusted — they are preset at the factory — often have a bimetal switch in the form of a little round disc that snaps back and forth in response to the correct temperature. Such preset thermostats are usually nonserviceable.

The detachable thermostats on heating appliances (skillets, electric frying pans, fondue pots, etc.) are often serviceable. A bimetal arm inside the control extends up into the probe that you insert into the appliance. The bimetal rod opens and closes a set of contacts to maintain an accurate temperature in the pan itself. When a problem arises in these controls, it is usually due to grease or vapor trapped in the control, or it is due to the control having been submerged in water. You can disassemble the housing of the control and clean it (with television tuner cleaner) to remove the unwanted material from the contacts. If the contacts are burned or pitted, clean them with an automotive point file, and then polish them to a bright finish before putting them back into operation.

If a detachable control unit proves to be defective, it is often possible to buy a replacement for the appliance. In fact, it often costs less to replace a defective component than to repair it, and it always costs less to replace one component than to buy a new appliance.

Heating appliances which use bimetal strips suffer the same basic problems that strike the detachable thermostatic controls, and you can service the strips in the same way. After inspecting the contacts — the two metal buttons on the thermostatic arm which carry the electrical current — clean and polish them to restore their smooth surface. Then, align the contacts and make sure that all of their linkages are free.

A few small heating appliances — and many

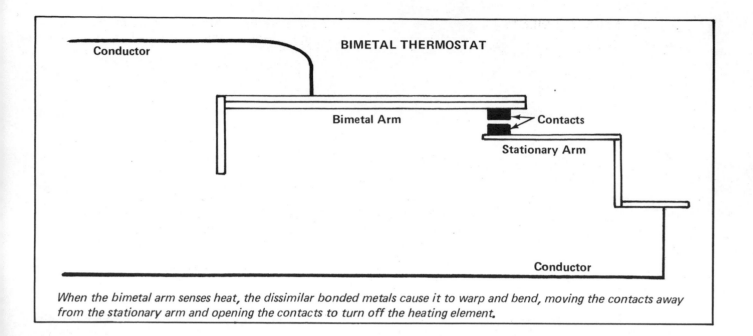

BIMETAL THERMOSTAT

Conductor

Bimetal Arm

Contacts

Stationary Arm

Conductor

When the bimetal arm senses heat, the dissimilar bonded metals cause it to warp and bend, moving the contacts away from the stationary arm and opening the contacts to turn off the heating element.

major appliances — use a sealed-tube thermostat to sense the temperature. The sealed-tube thermostat consists of a switch section and a long tube which is sealed at both ends. On the end within the switch, you will probably find a metallic bellows arrangement. The gas or liquid that is sealed in the tube expands as the heat rises. When the expansion reaches a certain point, it is sufficient to open the contact and turn off the heating element. When the gas or liquid cools sufficiently; the contacts close and turn the element on again. In essence, the

sealed-tube thermostat controls the heat within the appliance in the same manner as does the bimetal switch.

Quite frequently, thermostatic controls have a calibration screw which you can adjust if the temperature range varies significantly. Look for the screw under the thermostat knob, but do not attempt to calibrate a thermostat unless the heat varies more than 25 degrees from the control setting. In most cases, the calibration screw is marked with an arrow to indicate the direction you must turn it.

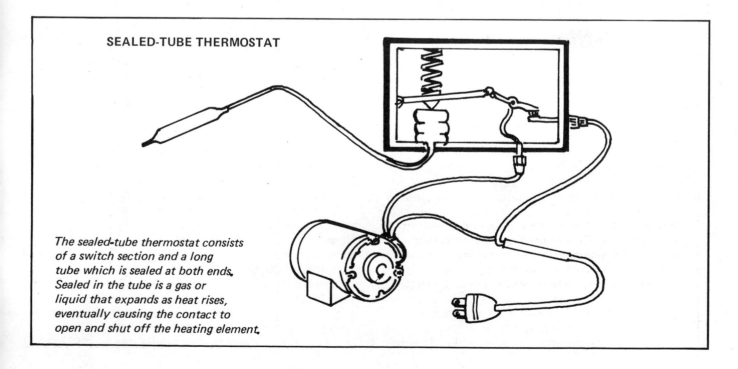

SEALED-TUBE THERMOSTAT

The sealed-tube thermostat consists of a switch section and a long tube which is sealed at both ends. Sealed in the tube is a gas or liquid that expands as heat rises, eventually causing the contact to open and shut off the heating element.

HEATING ELEMENTS

Heating elements in small appliances are made from nichrome wire. As its name suggests, the materials in the wire are nickel and chromium. Nichrome wire has excellent heating element characteristics. Since it has good properties of electrical resistance, it can be used at relatively high temperatures without burning out. The coil that you see supported from porcelain insulators on many heating appliances is, in fact, nichrome wire.

Other appliances utilize a sealed metal-sheathed heating element. The nichrome wire is still present, but it is enclosed within the metal sheath and insulated with a powder such as manganese. Such sealed units usually enjoy a long life because the nichrome is protected from oxidation, but when a defect occurs, the entire element must be replaced.

The same holds true for the open elements as well. Although you may be tempted merely to twist a broken wire back together (this solution will work for a short time), such a repair is usually short-lived. What you have done is to create a high resistance connection. Moreover, even assuming that you made a perfect connection at the breaking point, the element is usually in bad condition at other places along its length.

When replacing an open element, you can purchase nichrome wire in stock form, but be sure to get the diameter that you need. If you tell the supplier the wattage of your appliance, he can cut the wire into lengths to provide the correct wattage. Before you place the new element on its porcelain supports, take the old element out and stretch the new one to its correct length. Be careful when you stretch the new element, however. Were you to hold the new section directly in front of you, it could spring free and injure you. When you get the open element installed, make sure that it is supported firmly; it must not be allowed to sag. Moreover, make certain that the terminals where you attach the nichrome wire are bright and shiny. Frequently, you have to polish the terminals and/or the attaching nut with a file before tightening them.

CORDS AND WIRING

Cords and wiring used on heating appliances are of a special type; they are usually made of asbestos or fiberglass materials because they must be unaffected by the high temperatures inside heating appliances. Naturally, whenever you replace a cord or wire, be sure to check the appliance with a continuity tester to be certain that no wires or connections are touching the side of the cabinet causing a ground fault. If you should ever receive a

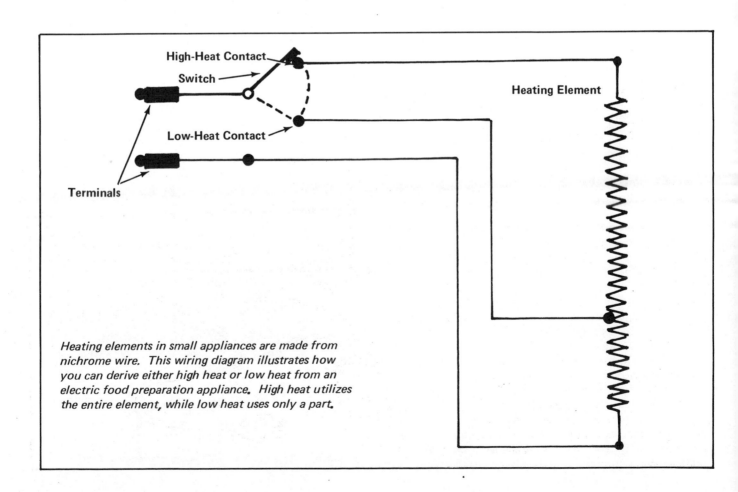

Heating elements in small appliances are made from nichrome wire. This wiring diagram illustrates how you can derive either high heat or low heat from an electric food preparation appliance. High heat utilizes the entire element, while low heat uses only a part.

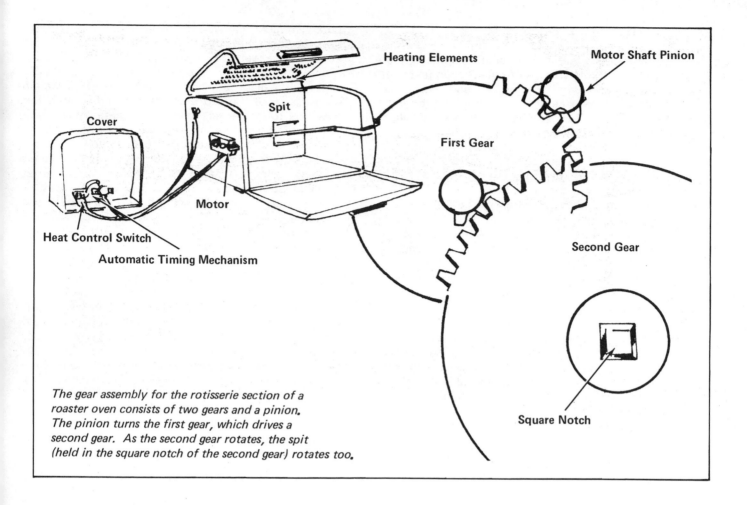

Cover

Heat Control Switch

Automatic Timing Mechanism

Motor

Spit

Heating Elements

First Gear

Motor Shaft Pinion

Second Gear

Square Notch

The gear assembly for the rotisserie section of a roaster oven consists of two gears and a pinion. The pinion turns the first gear, which drives a second gear. As the second gear rotates, the spit (held in the square notch of the second gear) rotates too.

shock from such an appliance, deenergize the device and do not attempt to use it again until you eliminate the defect.

Heating appliances that have a blower — like hair dryers or portable room heaters — should be kept free of lint. All passageways in such appliances must be clear. Many portable room heaters have a special bimetal switch to shut off the heating element when the temperature exceeds a predetermined safety level. If this switch should fail, it could also keep the heating element from operating. In addition to the special thermostat switch, portable electric heaters are required to have a "tipover switch." Often a weighted arm attached to the bimetal thermostat, the tipover switch opens the contacts and turns off the heating elements in the event that the heater winds up in a position other than its normal upright one.

Like other small appliances, heating appliances are usually held together by hidden screws and clips, but you should never detach any screws unless you can see that they will definitely aid you in getting to the inner works of the appliance. Look carefully under knobs, decals, and the outer trim on the appliance for the hidden screws and clips; in some cases, the trim itself may be the key to unlocking the puzzle. As you would do with any appliance, you

must unplug portable heating appliances before you inspect or repair them. You can safely check any electrical component in a portable heating appliance with a battery-powered continuity tester.

Basically, there are just two sections of a heating appliance that you need to know about: the

Toastmaster's Rotisserie/Oven-Broiler cleans itself.

The Ronson Deluxe Broiler/Oven features a positioning lever, enabling you to raise and lower the oven tray.

heating element itself and the control system that keeps the element working within the correct limits. The heat level, of course, varies according to the function of the particular appliance. To understand the appliance, merely examine these two sections. If you cannot discover any problem in the element or the control system, then by process of elimination you know that the trouble must lie with the wiring that connects the electrical circuit to the two basic sections. Applying these fundamentals to your heating appliance repair problems should make your work much easier.

ROASTER OVENS

The roaster oven is like a self-contained portable oven. The body is insulated from the outer cabinet with fiberglass, and the controls are usually mounted to one side. Sealed elements are the most common heat sources used in a roaster oven. Heat is radiated from the element both by direct radiation and by reflective heat from the polished oven liner.

A thermostat controls the heat in the roaster oven in much the same way as it does on your electric range. The thermostat may be a bimetal strip mounted near the oven cavity, or it may be a sealed-tube thermostat with the sensing tube mounted inside the oven body itself. Some ovens that have both upper and lower heating elements also have a switch to allow either element to operate independently of the other.

Many roaster ovens — and some open grills — have a rotisserie to turn portions of meat under the element for even broiling. The motor in a rotisserie unit is usually a shaded-pole type, with its speed greatly reduced by a gear train. In the center of the output gear is a socket, and the end of the spit fits into the socket and locks into position in the rotisserie rack.

If a heating element fails, you can replace it with a duplicate recommended by the manufacturer. Usually, the replacement element is designed and shaped to provide the right amount of heat within the allotted space. Before you actually connect the element to the wiring, though, you must do two things: Unplug the roaster, and make sure that all terminals are bright and shiny.

If the thermostat is a bimetal type and it ever fails to operate properly, check the contact points. Cleaning and polishing the contact points can often restore satisfactory operation. If the thermostat is erratic, however, it should be replaced. When you put in the new thermostat, moreover, you should install new insulation as well. Naturally, you should

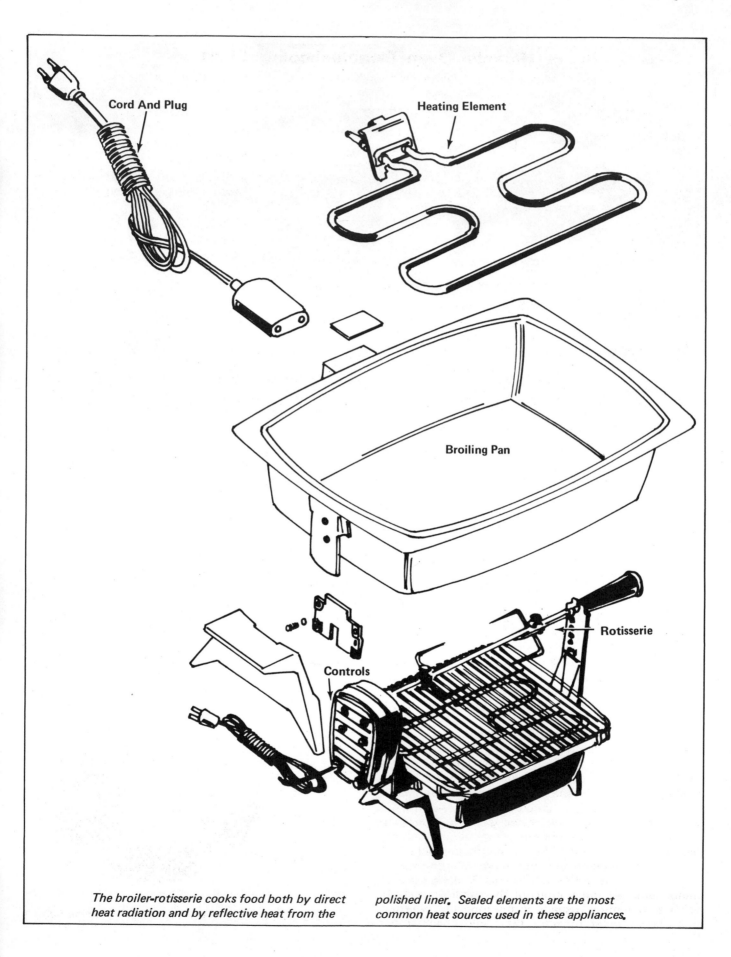

Cord And Plug

Heating Element

Broiling Pan

Rotisserie

Controls

The broiler-rotisserie cooks food both by direct heat radiation and by reflective heat from the polished liner. Sealed elements are the most common heat sources used in these appliances.

Roaster Oven Troubleshooting Chart

Caution: Unplug appliance before inspecting or repairing. Do not reconnect power until job is completed or while any wiring connections are exposed.

PROBLEMS	CAUSES	REPAIRS
Roaster oven does not go on	1. Bad on-off switch.	1. Replace the switch with one made by the manufacturer for your model.
	2. Heating element has an open wire.	2. Replace the element with one made by the manufacturer for your model.
Roaster oven gets too hot or not hot enough	1. Malfunctioning thermostat.	1. Check contact points; replacing them usually solves the problem.
Rotisserie will not turn	1. Loss of lubricant.	1. Remove the gears, clean them with a solvent, replace any that are bent or damaged, and relubricate with a light oil.
Roaster emits electrical shocks	1. Ground fault.	1. Locate the grounded component with a continuity tester, and either repair or replace it. Do not use the appliance as long as it has a ground fault.

also check the roaster oven with a continuity tester for ground faults before you put the appliance back to work once again.

COFFEEMAKERS

There are several types of coffeemakers to choose from in today's market. Basically, these appliances all accomplish their function in the same way: they pass water slowly through ground coffee, and then they keep the coffee warm until you serve it.

The brewer, probably the simplest part of a coffeemaker, consists of two containers placed one on top of the other. The bottom container, which holds the cold water, is heated by the coffeemaker's heating element. As a result, the water rises through a glass tube into the top container. When the bottom container reaches a predetermined temperature, a thermostat opens and turns off the circuit to the heating element. As the bottom container begins to cool, a slight vacuum is created which pulls the water gently through the coffee grounds in the top container back to the bottom container. A warming element maintains the coffee at serving temperature.

In the percolator, the most common type of coffeemaker, the coffee is placed in a basket atop a metal tube. At the bottom of this tube is a check valve arrangement, usually in the form of a washer, that allows water to enter the pump chamber but

prevents it from passing back out the bottom area of the tube. The heating element heats the pump chamber, though not necessarily the water within the tank itself. The small amount of water in the chamber gets hot very quickly and tends to rise up the tube; at the top it spills across the coffee in the basket and then seeps back into the reservoir below. Since more water must flow in to replace that which flowed out,

The GE 12-cup stainless steel coffeemaker is immersible.

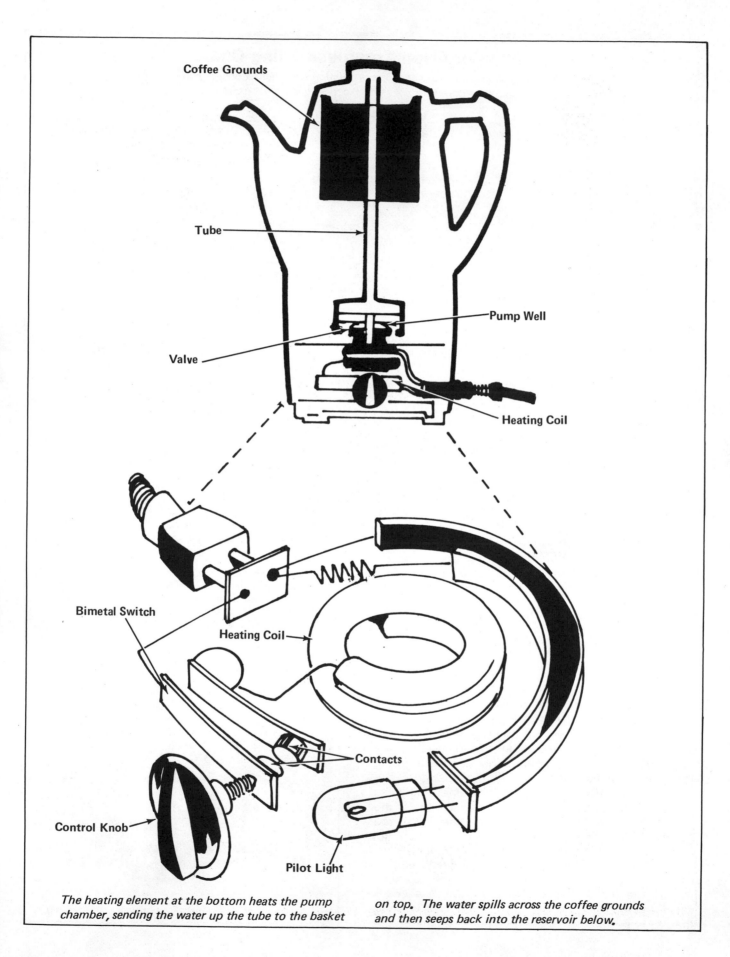

Coffee Grounds

Tube

Pump Well

Valve

Heating Coil

Bimetal Switch

Heating Coil

Contacts

Control Knob

Pilot Light

The heating element at the bottom heats the pump chamber, sending the water up the tube to the basket on top. The water spills across the coffee grounds and then seeps back into the reservoir below.

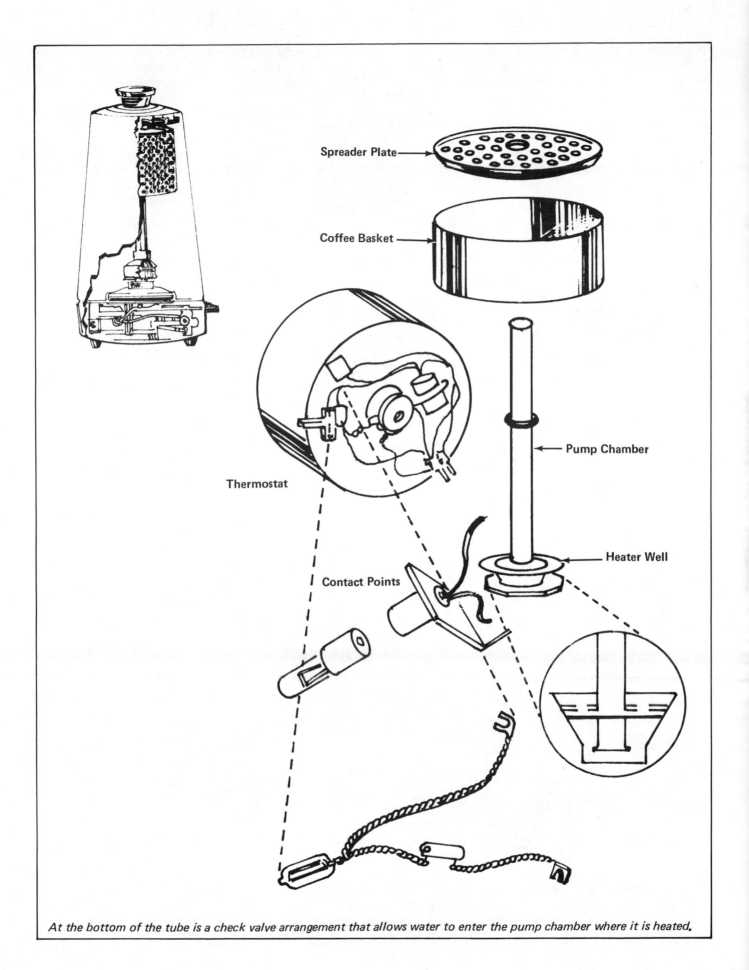

Spreader Plate

Coffee Basket

Thermostat

Pump Chamber

Contact Points

Heater Well

At the bottom of the tube is a check valve arrangement that allows water to enter the pump chamber where it is heated.

the check valve opens and the cycle is repeated.

The entire process happens very quickly once the coffeemaker reaches its percolation temperature. As the hot coffee falls back into the reservoir, its heat combines with the heat from the element to raise the temperature of the water within the tank. A bimetal thermostat senses this temperature and turns off the main heating element at a preset point. The preset point at which the thermostat shuts off the main heating element determines the strength of the coffee. If it were to open at a lower temperature, the percolation time would be reduced, and — as a result — the coffee would be weaker.

There is something new in coffeemakers called the drip-filter or single-pass coffeemaker. The drip-filter system heats the water in a separate reservoir, and it then passes the water up through a tube which is actually a spout. The coffee grounds, held in a filter above the server, receives the hot

Coffeemaker Troubleshooting Chart

Caution: Unplug appliance before inspecting or repairing. Do not reconnect power until job is completed or while any wiring connections are exposed.

PROBLEMS	CAUSES	REPAIRS
Coffeemaker does not heat	1. Faulty power cord connection.	1. Be sure power cord is firmly connected at terminal prongs and in wall socket.
	2. Bad power cord.	2. Unplug the cord and bend it back and forth over its length while testing with a continuity tester.
	3. Open heating element.	3. Test the percolator for continuity. Repair or replace a defective element.
	4. Open thermostat.	4. Test for continuity, and repair or replace if the thermostat is faulty.
Coffeemaker does not maintain heat	1. Incorrect thermostat setting.	1. Readjust and test the thermostat by placing a thermometer in percolator. With the thermostat set at its "medium" setting, the temperature should be about 212 degrees.
	2. Faulty thermostat.	2. Replace the thermostat.
Coffeemaker does not pump water	1. Clogged tube or well.	1. Clean out sediment.
	2. Bad washer in the base of the tube (washer assists in pumping water up the tube).	2. Replace the tube.
Bad tasting coffee	1. Dirty pot.	1. Clean the pot with electric percolator cleaner, available at hardware stores. Use as directed.
Water does not reach the top	1. Improper thermostat adjustment.	1. Readjust the thermostat.
	2. Inoperative main heating element.	2. Test the element for continuity and replace if defective.
Coffee boils over	1. Improperly positioned filter.	1. Position the filter correctly.
	2. Leaky gasket.	2. Replace any faulty gasket.

water as it pours from the spout. The brewed coffee then drips through the filter and into the server, which is heated by a warming element at the base of the coffeemaker.

Before you do anything to fix a broken coffeemaker, be sure to pull the plug and to leave the appliance disconnected all the time you are working on it. If you must remove the heating element from a percolator for any reason, be sure that you install a new gasket when you put the coffeemaker back together again. The gasket usually gets torn when you work with the element, and a torn gasket means a leaky coffeemaker.

Coffeemaker thermostats that get out of calibration can be corrected. Usually, you can reset the thermostat by turning a small adjusting screw, but a thermostat that is way off should be replaced. Some coffeemakers have disk-type bimetal thermostats which are not adjustable, however. Such thermostats, of course, prohibit you from simply dialing the coffee strength you desire. The only alternatives

you have are to alter the ratio of coffee to water or to replace the thermostat.

ELECTRIC TOASTERS

Toasters are devices which suspend bread near a heating element. When the toasting (or browning) is completed, most toasters bring the bread back out to where you can reach it, and then they turn off the heating elements.

When you place the bread in the toaster, it rests on a carriage separated from the heating elements by small wires. The wires serve as guides to hold the toast in position. When you press the knob to lower the toast, you also depress an internal spring mechanism. At the bottom of the spring mechanism is a latch that drops into position and holds the toast down. At the same time, the knob you press closes a switch to turn on the heating element. An exterior dial — usually marked "Darker" or "Lighter" — on the outside of the toaster allows

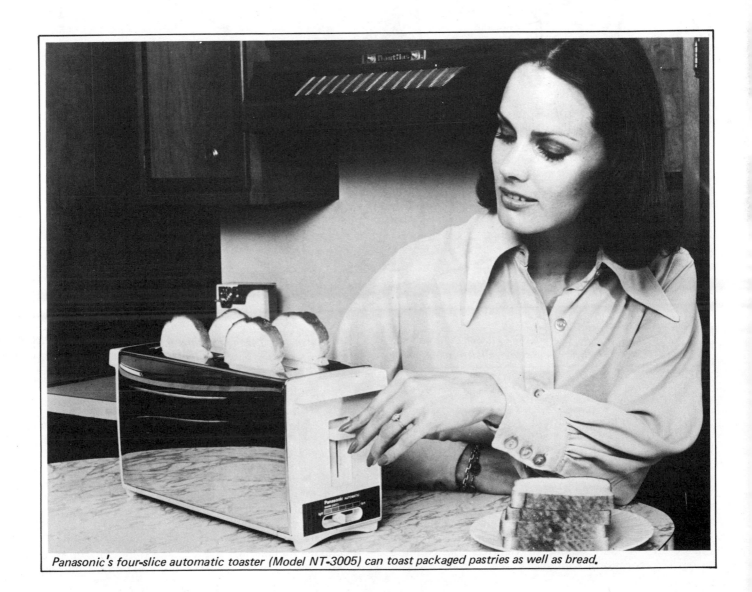

Panasonic's four-slice automatic toaster (Model NT-3005) can toast packaged pastries as well as bread.

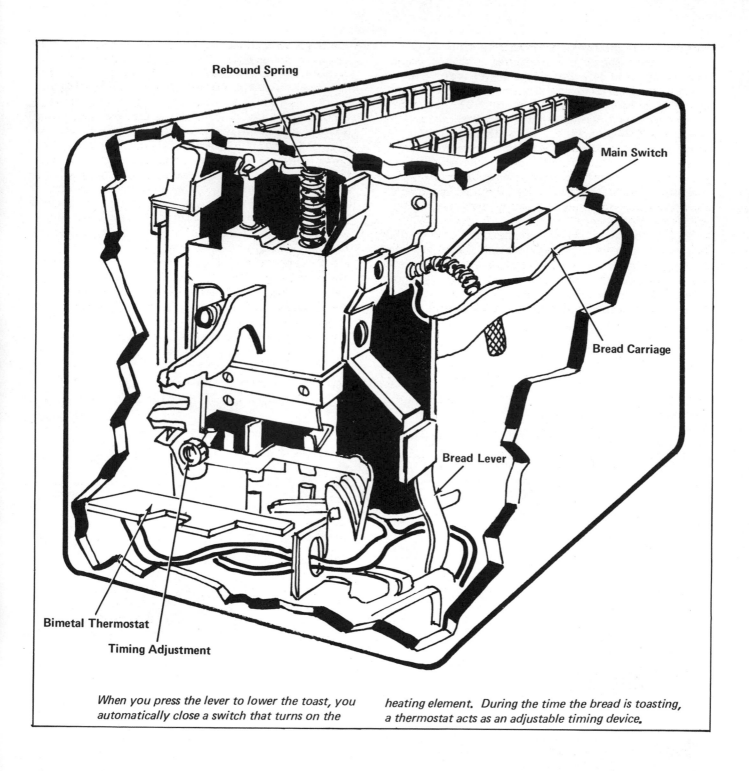

Rebound Spring

Main Switch

Bread Carriage

Bread Lever

Bimetal Thermostat

Timing Adjustment

When you press the lever to lower the toast, you automatically close a switch that turns on the heating element. During the time the bread is toasting, a thermostat acts as an adjustable timing device.

you to adjust the toasting time.

The heating elements in a toaster are the open type. Therefore, never use a metal object — such as a fork or a knife — to move a slice of bread or make any sort of adjustments. If you were to come in contact with one of the elements (even when the toaster was not in operation), you could receive a dangerous or even fatal shock. To clear a jammed toaster, unplug it, turn it upside-down, and use a plastic or wooden object to remove the jammed bread. In addition, appliances with open heating elements can suffer from fault grounds. If you ever get a shock from a toaster, take it out of service and do not use it again until you fix the fault.

During the period when the bread is toasting, a thermostat (or, in some cases, a clock motor arrangement) acts as a timing device. Regardless of the type of sensor that your toaster possesses, the action is the same. The heat causes the bimetal switch to bend, unlatching the mechanism. When the mechanism unlatches, the carriage begins its upward travel. The switch turns off the heating elements, and the bread pops out the top of the toaster.

The old cartoon depicting bread popping several feet out from the toaster can indeed be a reality. On the back of the toaster there is a shock-absorber mechanism to prevent the carriage from rising too rapidly, but if this mechanism fails, the toast can really take off.

Toasters usually require some maintenance, but you must remember to unplug your toaster before you inspect or repair it. Again, never insert anything into the top of the toaster without first unplugging it. Even after you unplug the toaster, use only a small blunt wooden object or other type of nonconductor. In addition, stay away from the heating elements. Touching or applying force to the heating elements can damage them, or even cause them to fail.

The most important preventive maintenance you can do is to brush away crumbs that accumulate around and under the toaster. Most units have a crumb tray which you can lower and remove from the bottom of the toaster. If your toaster lacks a crumb tray, use a long soft brush three or four times a year (depending upon usage) to clear the crumbs away.

Since the housing of a toaster completely surrounds the mechanism, this is one appliance that can be tricky to put back together. If it should become necessary to remove the housing, be sure to note the position of each knob and screw as you remove it. Generally, you have to take off the two end housings before you can remove the main housing itself.

WAFFLE IRONS

Modern electric waffle irons have evolved from the heavy cast-iron griddles that used to be placed on wood-burning stoves. Today, an electric heating element serves as the heat source, and

Toaster Troubleshooting Chart

Caution: Unplug appliance before inspecting or repairing. Do not reconnect power until job is completed or while any wiring connections are exposed.

PROBLEMS	CAUSES	REPAIRS
Toaster elements do not heat	1. No voltage at receptacle, or a defective cord.	1. Plug another appliance into the receptacle. If the receptacle works, check the toaster's cord and terminals. Replace a defective cord, but use only heat-resistant cord on your toaster.
	2. Defective thermostat or switch.	2. Check both the thermostat and switch with a continuity tester and replace any defective parts.
	3. Heating element open.	3. Check the element with a continuity tester and replace it if defective.
Uneven toasting	1. Moisture content of bread may be uneven.	1. Try other types of bread.
	2. One heating element is not operating.	2. Check all heating elements with a continuity tester. Replace as necessary.
Toast does not pop up	1. Linkage binding.	1. Clean toaster thoroughly and inspect linkage for binding. Check for broken spring, and replace as required.
Toast burns	1. Thermostat defective.	1. Check thermostat and replace it if necessary.
Toaster emits electrical shocks	1. Ground fault in heating element.	1. Test with a continuity tester and replace the defective component or replace the toaster. Do not use a toaster that has a ground fault.

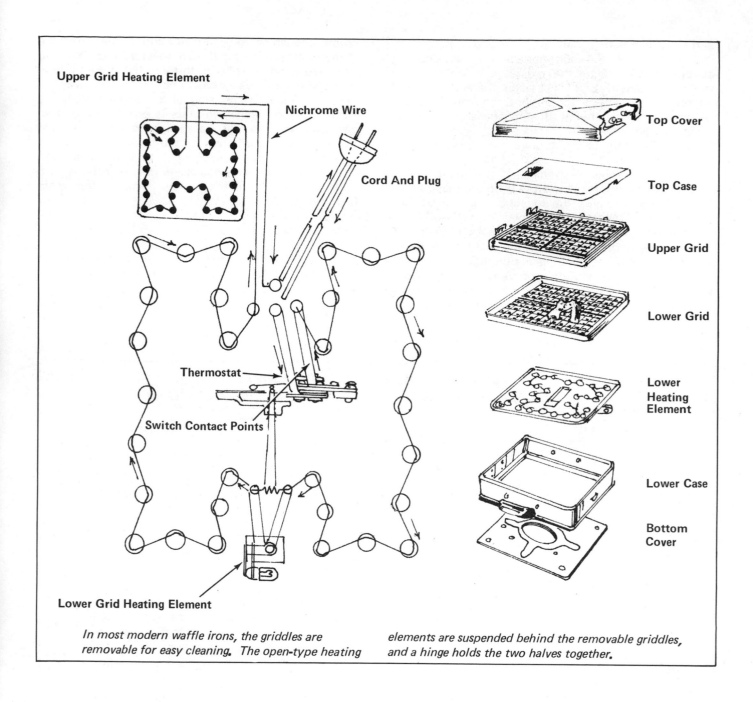

Upper Grid Heating Element

Nichrome Wire

Cord And Plug

Thermostat

Switch Contact Points

Lower Grid Heating Element

Top Cover

Top Case

Upper Grid

Lower Grid

Lower Heating Element

Lower Case

Bottom Cover

In most modern waffle irons, the griddles are removable for easy cleaning. The open-type heating elements are suspended behind the removable griddles, and a hinge holds the two halves together.

heavy aluminum castings transfer the heat quickly from the element to the waffle batter. A thermostat, usually of the bimetal type, regulates the temperature to provide even and controlled cooking.

In most modern waffle irons, the griddles are removable for cleaning; and in some cases, they are also reversible: the waffle griddle is on one side and a sandwich grill is on the other. The open-type heating elements are suspended behind the removable griddles, and a hinge holds the two halves — top and bottom — together.

Frequently, you will find waffle irons that have a light to signal when the unit is at the proper cooking temperature. Sometimes, this signal light is a bulb which is connected across the thermostat contacts. When the contacts are closed, the current flows through the elements. When the contacts are open, the current flows through the lamp, causing it to glow. Often, the waffle iron has just a jewel glass eye which allows you to see the glow of the heating element. Although not a technologically sophisticated design, such an eye can be an effective indicator. As the waffle iron reaches the proper temperature, the thermostat opens and the light turns off.

Generally, you can adjust the thermostat by turning a knob or moving a slide. The knob or slide adjusts the tension on the contacts, and thereby determines the temperature at which the contacts will open and close. The higher the temperature,

Farberware's Waffler & Grill has reversible griddles.

even some of the internal wiring that links these two components in your waffle iron. Be sure to use high-resistance wire when you are replacing either an internal wire or the external line cord.

Since there is a hinge holding the two halves of the waffle iron together, there must be passageway between the upper and lower sections for the wiring that carries current to each element. The connecting line is often enclosed within a flexible metal coil which prevents damage to the exposed wire, but over a long period of time the wire can be flexed so much that the conductors break inside the insulation. In such a case, you should remove the broken wire and replace it with heat-resistant wire of the same type.

PORTABLE ELECTRIC HEATERS

Electric heaters are relatively simple devices, consisting of a heating element suspended from porcelain insulators, a reflective surface, a thermostat (usually the bimetal type), and — quite frequently — an electric fan to increase the heat output into the room. Most heaters are designed to pass air behind the reflective surface in the area of the heating element, thereby transmitting heat into the room by radiation from the reflective surface as

naturally, the browner the waffle will be when baking is completed.

Problems that afflict waffle irons are similar to the problems that can strike any appliances that use heating elements and bimetal thermostats. You may have to replace an element or a thermostat or

Waffle Iron Troubleshooting Chart

Caution: Unplug appliance before inspecting or repairing. Do not reconnect power until job is completed or while any wiring connections are exposed.

PROBLEMS	CAUSES	REPAIRS
Waffle iron fails to heat	1. Open circuit.	1. Test power cord for continuity. Replace if defective. 2. Test elements for continuity. Replace if element wire is broken. 3. Check thermostat for dirty contact points, bent blades, broken wires. Repair if possible; replace thermostat if repair is impossible.
Waffle iron gets too hot	1. Contact points welded together, causing elements to stay on all the time.	1. Pry contacts apart and clean them or install a new thermostat.
Waffle iron fails to get hot enough	1. Thermostat not adjusted properly.	1. Readjust the thermostat.
Waffle iron emits electrical shocks	1. Ground fault.	1. Locate the ground fault with a continuity tester, and replace defective component or buy a new waffle iron. Do not use a waffle iron that possesses a ground fault.

Dominion Custom Portable Heaters feature an adjustable thermostat, fan-forced heat, and automatic shut-off.

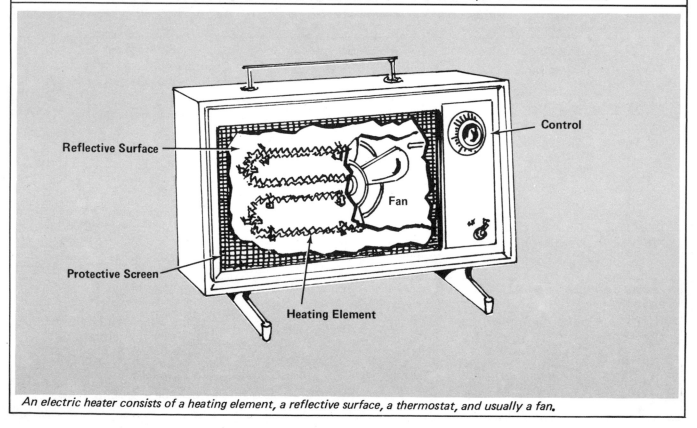

Reflective Surface

Control

Fan

Protective Screen

Heating Element

An electric heater consists of a heating element, a reflective surface, a thermostat, and usually a fan.

well as through the convection of the heated air from behind the reflector.

Electric heaters must be kept free from lint and dust. Clean heaters not only operate more efficiently, but they also eliminate one possible fire hazard in your home. Before you ever attempt to clean your heater (or service it in any other way), make certain the heater is unplugged. Once you are sure it is disconnected, you can vacuum away any lint, but take care not to damage the element(s).

Always test the heater for fault grounds, using a continuity tester, when you finish repairs, and never let the heater element come in contact with any part of the housing. Lubricate the fan motor every year, and use a damp cloth to clean the polished surface of the reflector; it should be as shiny as possible to assure maximum efficiency from the heater.

Since portable electric room heaters operate at a relatively high current, you should avoid using extension cords with them. Place the unit as close to the receptacle as you possibly can.

HAIR DRYERS

Hand-held hair dryers and bonnet-style hair dryers operate in basically the same manner. A fan forces air across the heating element — located

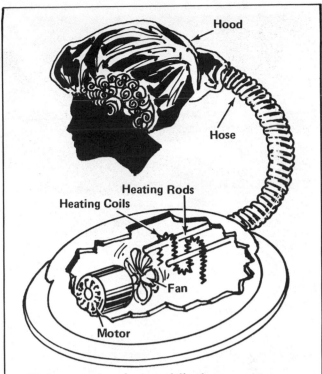

All dryers operate in essentially the same way: a fan forces air across the heating element and then out through a nozzle or tube to your hair.

Electric Heaters Troubleshooting Chart

Caution: Unplug appliance before inspecting or repairing. Do not reconnect power until job is completed or while any wiring connections are exposed.

PROBLEMS	CAUSES	REPAIRS
Heater fails to start	1. No voltage to receptacle.	1. Test the receptacle with a lamp or another appliance.
	2. Defective cord.	2. Replace the cord with heat-resistant wiring of sufficient capacity.
	3. Open thermostat.	3. Test with continuity tester and clean. Replace thermostat if defective.
	4. Heater not level.	4. Be sure that the heater is level.
Insufficient heat	1. Clogged air passages.	1. Clear passages.
	2. Tarnished or dirty reflector.	2. Clean and polish reflector.
	3. Extension cord of insufficient capacity.	3. Plug heater directly into receptacle.
Heater emits electrical shocks	1. Grounded component in heater.	1. Locate and replace defective component or replace heater. Do not use a heater that possesses a grounded component.

The Dominion Deluxe Blower/Styler has switch settings for cool, low, medium, and high heat.

Hair Dryers Troubleshooting Chart

Caution: Unplug appliance before inspecting or repairing. Do not reconnect power until job is completed or while any wiring connections are exposed.

PROBLEMS	CAUSES	REPAIRS
Hair dryer fails to run at all	1. No voltage to receptacle.	1. Test the receptacle with a lamp or another appliance.
	2. Defective cord or plug.	2. Replace cord or plug with proper type.
	3. Defective switch.	3. Check with continuity tester and replace defective switch.
Hair dryer overheats	1. Motor not operating.	1. Check motor for binding and proper electrical operation. Replace if defective.
	2. Air passageways blocked or clogged.	2. Check passageways. Check air intake.
No heat or insufficient heat	1. Heating element(s) open.	1. Check with continuity tester and replace if necessary.
	2. Safety thermostat open.	2. Check thermostat when cool, replace if open.
Noisy operation	1. Fan binding or striking cabinet.	1. Check and clean fan assembly.

within the base (or within the nozzle) of the hair dryer — and out the nozzle or tube. Bonnet-type hair dryers have a tube which leads to the bonnet itself, and the warm air circulates through the bonnet, removing moisture as it goes.

Hair dryers must contain a safety-limit thermostat to shut the unit off in case it should overheat, which could happen if the blower motor failed to operate or if the air passageways were to become blocked. A safety limit usually takes the form of a small preset bimetal thermostat, and it is often included as part of the heating element.

Many hair dryers have a switch instead of an adjustable thermostat to provide heat ranges. The switch controls the heat by connecting and disconnecting the elements in the circuit. When the switch is set to the low position, for example, the blower motor and the low-wattage heating element work together. In the middle position, the high-wattage heater operates in conjunction with the blower. In the high position, both high- and low-wattage elements work with the blower running. Only in the air position does the blower run with no heating element working with it.

Styling combs operate in much the same manner. A miniature heating element and blower motor (contained in the unit's handle) pull room air in at one end and force hot air out the other where the comb or styling attachment is located.

Before you inspect, test, or service any kind of hair dryer, be sure that the unit is unplugged. When you are certain that it is disconnected, look for the small screens which protect the hair dryer's air inlet. You must vacuum these screens regularly to keep them free of hair, dust, and lint. If you own a bonnet-type hair dryer, take every precaution to prevent the tube (or hose) from becoming kinked or

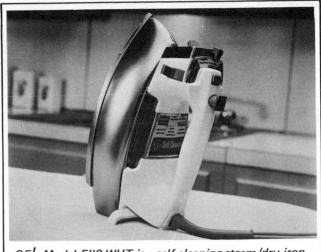

GE's Model FII0 WHT is a self-cleaning steam/dry iron.

blocked. Follow these basic rules of preventive maintenance, and you should obtain good service and long life from your hair dryer.

ELECTRIC IRONS

The electric iron is another example of an appliance that has evolved from a pre-electrical-age device. Gone are the heavy metal units that had no built-in heat source, much less any convenience features. Today's electric iron not only provides a complete range of temperatures to care for all sorts of modern fabrics, but in most cases it also acts as a steam iron.

The heating element of most electric irons is cast in the base or sole plate of the iron. Since its

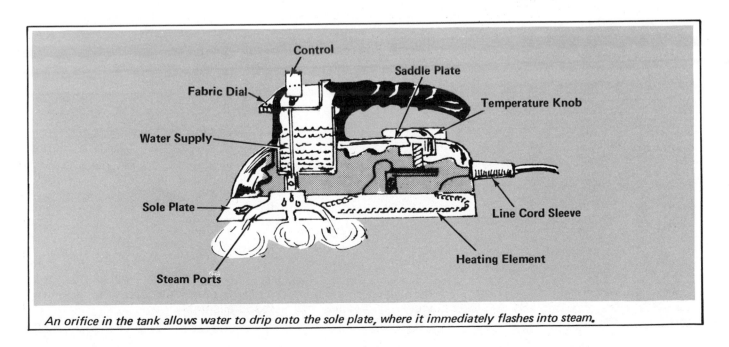

An orifice in the tank allows water to drip onto the sole plate, where it immediately flashes into steam.

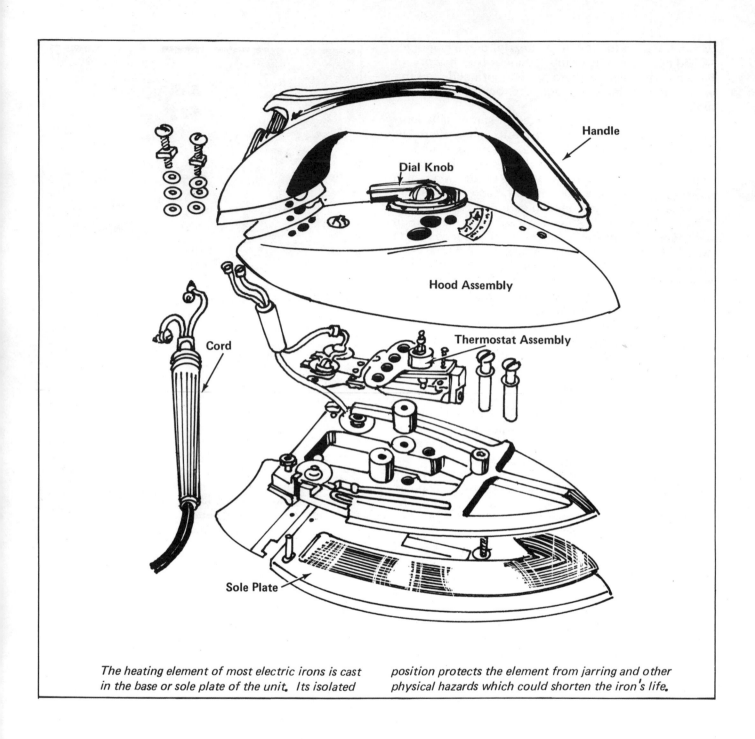

Handle

Dial Knob

Hood Assembly

Thermostat Assembly

Cord

Sole Plate

The heating element of most electric irons is cast in the base or sole plate of the unit. Its isolated position protects the element from jarring and other physical hazards which could shorten the iron's life.

isolated position protects the heating element from hazards — like jarring — the heating element seldom fails. If for some reason it should fail, however, the heating element in an iron cannot be replaced or repaired.

The thermostat — the bimetal type — is located above the sole plate. It senses the temperature directly from the plate, and then it turns the element on and off to maintain the correct temperature. In most steam irons, a water tank is also mounted above the plate. An orifice in the tank allows water to drip onto the sole plate, where it immediately flashes into steam. The vapor is then forced out orifices in the base of the sole plate and onto your clothing.

One of the most common maladies to afflict an electric iron is a broken cord. Although the cord is meant to be flexed a great deal during normal usage, it can become frayed or the internal wires can break over a long period of time. Always replace a defective iron cord promptly, but make sure that the cord you purchase as a replacement is intended for use on an iron. Such cords are available at most manufacturers' parts outlets as well as at many hardware stores.

Unplug the iron before you replace the cord

or perform any other maintenance or repair task. You can generally replace the cord by removing a small insulating cover located in the base of the handle where the cord enters the iron. In most cases, two screws hold this cover in place. With the cover removed, you will see the terminals for the wiring connections. Sometimes, the connector is a single screw which passes through eyelets in the new iron cord, while in other irons there is a connector which clips onto the terminals. Inspect your iron before you purchase a new cord to see which type of connector your iron uses. Be sure you get a cord that fits without your having to modify or replace the terminals. All connectors, of course, should be bright and shiny.

Many iron problems result from mineral deposits in the water clogging the steam passageways. In its early stages, such clogging produces sputtering noises and it deposits brown substances on your clothing. Several commercial iron cleaners are available for cleaning out the mineral deposits; just make sure that you get one that is recommended by the manufacturer of the iron you own.

The best solution to the mineral deposit problem, however, is preventive maintenance. Use only distilled water (or rain water) in your iron, and filter the water through a cloth before you put it in the iron. If you empty the iron after each use, moreover, you can minimize the deposit buildup. The heat from the iron will vaporize any moisture that remains after you empty the water tank.

Naturally, if you abuse your iron, it will fail to perform as well or as long as it should. For example, irons placed on unstable ironing boards frequently wind up on the floor. In addition, be very careful when ironing to avoid dropping the appliance, and be sure that you stay close enough to the receptacle to avoid straining or pulling on the cord. If you should happen to drop the iron, however, and the handle were to break, you can generally use epoxy cement to bond the broken pieces back together again. If the handle breaks beyond repair, though, you can generally install a replacement handle.

If a fall damages the iron badly or if you spot any water leakage, the seals on the tank may be warped or out of place. Generally, it is less expensive to replace the iron than to repair it in such instances — even if you are doing all the work yourself. Leakage of vapor from the steam tank, though, does not mean that you must buy a new iron, although such leakage can sometimes cause corrosion of the thermostat contacts. If this happens, clean the contacts with an automotive point file, and then polish the contacts before you put the iron back together again.

If you ever receive a shock from an iron, take it out of service at once, and be sure to locate and eliminate the electrical problem before you use the iron again. If the problem is a ground fault in the heating element, do not attempt to fix the appliance. Instead, buy yourself a new iron.

ELECTRIC BLANKETS AND HEATING PADS

The electric blanket is composed of a lightweight blanket with very fine flexible wires woven between two layers of the material. Since these wires possess high resistance, the heat output is relatively low — just enough to provide comfort-

Electric Irons Troubleshooting Chart

Caution: Unplug appliance before inspecting or repairing. Do not reconnect power until job is completed or while any wiring connections are exposed.

PROBLEMS	CAUSES	REPAIRS
Iron fails to heat	1. No voltage at receptacle.	1. Check receptacle with a table lamp.
	2. Defective cord.	2. Check cord at plug. Use heat-resistant cord for replacement.
	3. Thermostat or heating element open.	3. Check with continuity tester, and replace defective parts.
Water spurts from sole plate	1. Iron clogged.	1. Disassemble and clean.
Iron overheats	1. Thermostat defective.	1. Replace thermostat.
Iron emits electrical shocks	1. Grounded line or component in iron.	1. Locate and replace the grounded component or replace the iron. Never use an iron that possesses a fault ground.

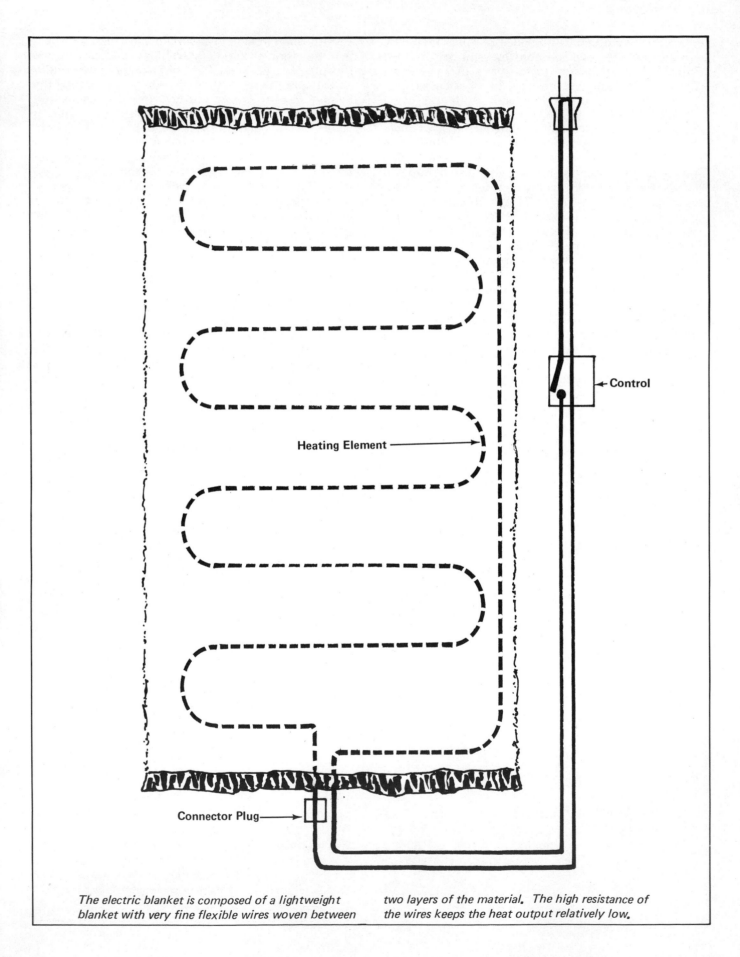

Control

Heating Element

Connector Plug

The electric blanket is composed of a lightweight blanket with very fine flexible wires woven between two layers of the material. The high resistance of the wires keeps the heat output relatively low.

able warmth. Special thermostats are built into the blanket at intervals to turn off the wires in case they overheat.

The electric blanket control contains a thermostat and a small compensating heater that goes on whenever the blanket heating elements are energized. Thus, the bimetal thermostat responds both to the room temperature and to the action of the heating elements. When you turn the dial on the control, you adjust the tension on the bimetal. A higher setting means that the heaters are on for a longer time, raising the temperature of the blanket.

Be sure to follow the manufacturer's instructions for placing the blanket on the bed. The plug connector at the foot of the blanket should be located on the outside rather than underneath the blanket for reasons of safety — that location prevents you from inadvertently touching the plug. Since you must be very careful not to damage the internal thermostats or the delicate wiring, you should never place packages or objects on a bed covered with an electric blanket. In addition, you should avoid using bedspreads or other blankets with an electric blanket. The other bed covers can throw off the electric blanket's temperature-control mechanism.

If the control mechanism ever fails to operate, try cleaning the contacts by passing a strip of paper between them. That should remove any oily film or insulating material from the contacts.

An electric heating pad is intended to provide a more intense heat in a more concentrated area than an electric blanket is designed to do. The fabric of an electric heating pad is a heavy (often rubberized) material, and two elements — with high and low wattage — generate the heat. A switch attached to the line cord turns these elements on and off to provide the degree of heat you desire. The low position turns on the low-wattage heating element, the medium position activates the high wattage heating element, and the high position energizes both heating elements. A safety thermostat is usually built into the pad to shut off the unit in case it should overheat.

If a heating pad element fails, you can still use the pad at the other heat settings. You should not, however, ever try to open a heating pad (or an electric blanket) to try to fix a defective heating element.

Electric Blankets And Heating Pads Troubleshooting Chart

Caution: Unplug appliance before inspecting or repairing. Do not reconnect power until job is completed or while any wiring connections are exposed.

PROBLEMS	CAUSES	REPAIRS
Blanket fails to heat	1. No voltage to receptacle.	1. Check receptacle with a table lamp; replace fuse, reset circuit breaker, or repair receptacle.
	2. Contacts in control not closing.	2. Clean contact surface with strip of paper.
	3. Poor connection at blanket connector.	3. Check for proper connection.
	4. Open thermostat in blanket.	4. Not repairable. Replace blanket.
	5. Open element in blanket.	5. Not repairable. Replace blanket.
Blanket overheating or not heating enough	1. Control placed in area not relative to temperature in remainder of room.	1. Move control. Avoid drafty or cooler areas or areas in front of a heating duct.
	2. Control not calibrated correctly.	2. Look for calibration screw on bimetal strip. Adjust only slightly.
Heating pad fails to heat on all settings	1. One element out.	1. Check with continuity tester. If open, element cannot be repaired, but pad may be usable on other heat ranges.
	2. Open contact surface in control.	2. Inspect control. Repair connection or clean contact surface.

Chapter Three

Motorized Small Appliances

Motorized small appliances are usually powered by either a shaded-pole or a universal motor, depending upon the starting force (or torque) required. In most cases, some sort of reduction drive lowers the motor's speed to that which is necessary for the appliance to function properly. Often, a worm gear is machined into the output shaft of the motor to rotate a drive gear or reduction gear train. Most appliances use tapped windings in the fields of their motors to accomplish speed control, but certain appliances — such as food mixers — utilize a type of mechanical governor on the rotor shaft.

The first step in servicing a motorized small appliance is to pinpoint the cause of the trouble. The best way of diagnosing malfunctions is to observe the symptoms. If you decide that you must disassemble the appliance before you can repair it, you will have to look closely to find the screws and clips which hold these devices together. Due to the manufacturers' styling preferences, the screws and clips are often hidden under trim pieces or under the rubber feet at the bottom of the appliance.

If the fault lies within the motor unit itself, first determine the type of motor used and then consult the chapter dealing with appliance motors to obtain the servicing information you need. If the problem is within the drive train, you can usually see the trouble spot. Make sure that the appliance is unplugged, and then remove the housing or cover. Now, turn the motor with your finger and watch closely for signs of chipping or stripping as the gears revolve. The gears on many appliances — particularly mixers — are timed to turn in such a way as to avoid damage to the mechanism or attachments. Before removing gears from a small appliance, therefore, check the timing marks; they must be aligned. When replacing the gears, moreover, make certain that the timing marks go back in the same position as they were before you removed the gears.

Many portable motorized appliances that are designed for food preparation can suffer from the effects of certain ingredients. Flour dust can coat the inside of a mixer and produce a mechanical failure later on. Liquids can spill around the cutting edges of an electric can opener, causing the appliance to bind and become inoperative. Look for such problems when diagnosing food preparation appliance malfunctions, and be sure to clean away any residue if you have to go inside the appliance. Such cleaning by itself can often restore the unit's operating efficiency.

Observe good work habits when you are working with small appliances. Place a protective surface (like a towel) on the workbench, but never work on a carpet. The tiny springs of a motorized small appliance can disappear forever if they drop from the work surface into the nap of a carpet. Use the right tools for the job: match screwdrivers with the screws, and use the tool in such a way as to prevent slippage. Beware of sharp edges on metal stampings, and, of course, be sure that the appliance is unplugged before you attempt to perform any service on it.

FOOD MIXERS

Food mixers possess a universal motor to turn two drive gears. Incorporated into each drive gear is a socket to which the beaters attach; a spring clip locks each beater in place. The drive gears, which are called pinions, rotate in opposite directions. To prevent the beaters from becoming entangled with each other as they turn, the drive gears always have timing marks of some sort. Look for these marks and note their position well before disassembling a mixer. Sometimes a sketch can be

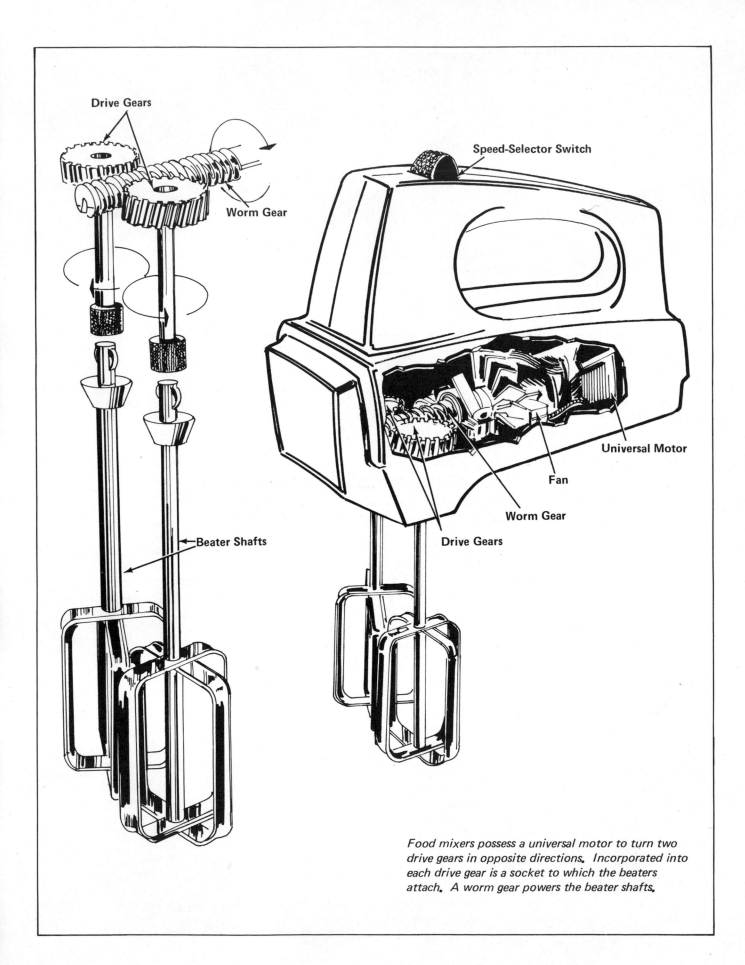

Drive Gears

Worm Gear

Speed-Selector Switch

Universal Motor

Fan

Worm Gear

Drive Gears

Beater Shafts

Food mixers possess a universal motor to turn two drive gears in opposite directions. Incorporated into each drive gear is a socket to which the beaters attach. A worm gear powers the beater shafts.

very helpful in reassembling the drive gears properly.

Most mixers have a small fan built onto the motor; the fan is designed to pull cooling air through the housing. The fan, however, can also pull food particles into the mixer which then coat the electric components and cause the mechanical parts to bind. Whenever you open a mixer for a service inspection, be sure to brush away the food residue.

The speed control mechanism is an important part of a mixer. If you see a number of wires where the motor field is connected into the circuit — or if the switch has three or more "click" positions — then you know that the mixer employs a tapped field winding.

Sometimes, you open a mixer and see a mechanical device attached to the end of the armature opposite the worm gear. The mechanical device is a governor arrangement which opens and closes a set of contacts to provide a variety of positive motor speeds. Frequently, you can detect the presence of a governor arrangement simply by listening to the sound of the mixer at low speeds. A sound similar to a "miss" is a sure indicator. In effect, that is what the sound is. The governor causes the contacts to open, breaking the circuit to

If you open the housing of a lightweight mixer, you will see a governor arrangement for speed control.

the motor when the mixer reaches a particular speed. As the motor slows down, the contacts close very quickly to maintain the speed at a particular level. If you move the speed control knob to a higher position, the speed required to open the contacts increases. In the top position, the contacts are

Food Mixers Troubleshooting Chart

Caution: Unplug appliance before inspecting or repairing. Do not reconnect power until job is completed or while any wiring connections are exposed.

PROBLEMS	CAUSES	REPAIRS
Mixer fails to run	1. No power at the receptacle.	1. Check the condition of the receptacle with a table lamp.
	2. Defective plug and/or cord.	2. Check the condition of the plug and cord, and replace if necessary.
	3. Defective motor brushes.	3. Check the condition of the brushes in a universal motor. Replace the brushes if they are less than 1/4-inch long.
	4. Defective switch contacts.	4. Check the condition of the switch contacts on the governor. Sometimes, cleaning away food residue can remedy the problem.
Mixer cannot be regulated for speed	1. Defective speed control.	1. Check the speed control linkage and contacts.
	2. Electrical short.	2. Check for a short in the speed control capacitor unit.
Mixer generates loud noises and/or the beaters fail to revolve	1. Defective drive train.	1. Check for broken or damaged gears, and observe the timing marks when installing replacement gears. Check the beaters for signs of damage.

KitchenAid's 3KF-602l comes with a dough-mixing device.

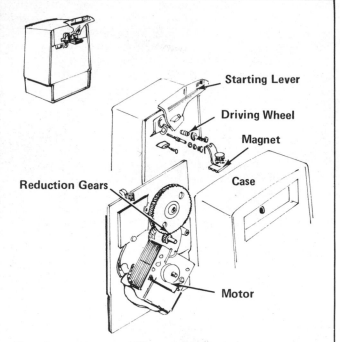

Starting Lever

Driving Wheel

Magnet

Reduction Gears

Case

Motor

Electric can openers utilize a shaded-pole motor and a reduction drive to turn a sprocket gear (or driving wheel) located on the side of the housing. The gear's teeth grip the top of the can and turn it against the cutter.

usually locked shut, and the motor turns at its top speed. If a fault exists within the speed-control mechanism, look for binding in the governor component.

Some mixers also have a resistor to provide low speed control, and most mixers with governors have a capacitor attached across the contact points to reduce radio interference and arcing as the governor contacts open and close. You can usually remove a faulty resistor or capacitor by clipping it out of its terminal connection.

ELECTRIC CAN OPENERS

Electric can openers use a shaded-pole motor and a reduction drive to turn a sprocket gear (or driving wheel) located on the side of the housing. After you place the can in the gear, you pull the locking handle down to pierce the can and hold it firmly. Pressing down on the locking handle also starts the motor. As the sprocket gear turns, the teeth grip the top of the can and turn it against the cutter which opens the can. Usually, a magnetic device rests on the lid to hold it when the cutter completes its operations. Some can openers require that you hold the handle in a depressed position to keep the motor running and the can rotating, while other units have a switch connected to the piercing mechanism. After the top is cut away, the switch-type can opener shuts off automatically.

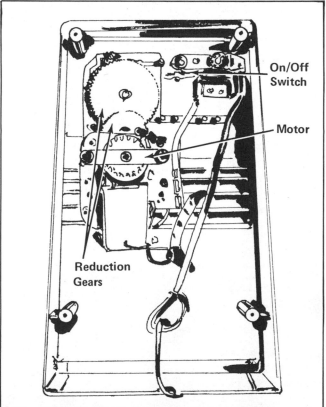

On/Off Switch

Motor

Reduction Gears

View of the backside of an electric can opener shows how motor power is reduced via a reduction gear setup.

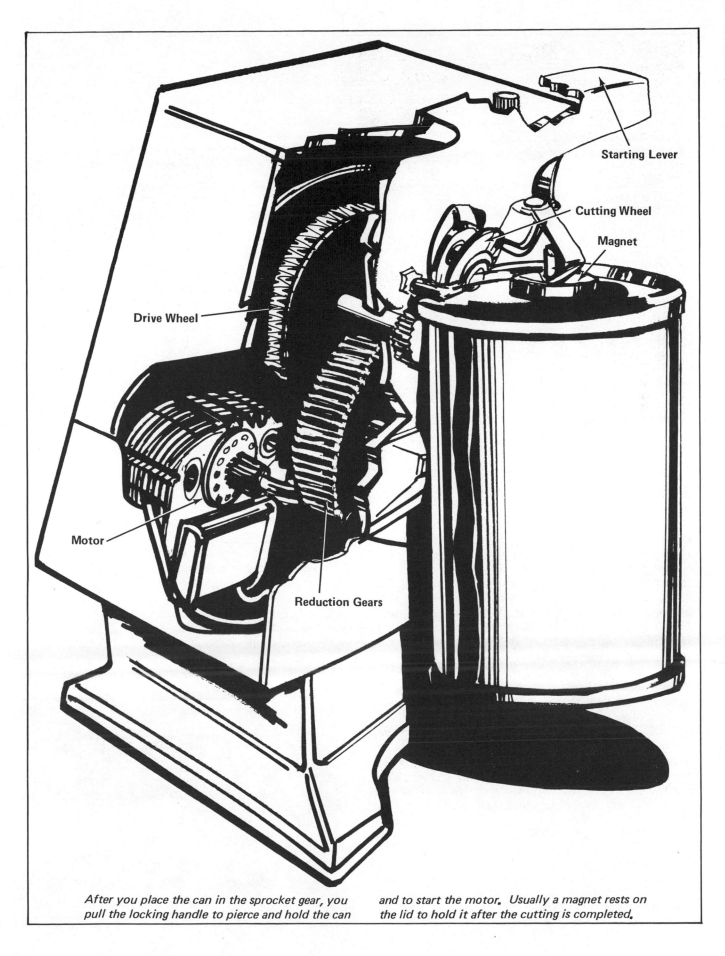

Starting Lever

Cutting Wheel

Magnet

Drive Wheel

Motor

Reduction Gears

After you place the can in the sprocket gear, you pull the locking handle to pierce and hold the can and to start the motor. Usually a magnet rests on the lid to hold it after the cutting is completed.

Electric Can Opener Troubleshooting Chart

Caution: Unplug appliance before inspecting or repairing. Do not reconnect power until job is completed or while any wiring connections are exposed.

PROBLEMS	CAUSES	REPAIRS
Blade skips instead of cutting	1. Dirt in blade.	1. Remove the cutting assembly, and soak it in hot soapy water until the dirt floats away.
Can opener fails to turn on	1. Broken receptacle.	1. Test the receptacle with another appliance or a table lamp, and make the necessary repairs.
	2. Damaged power cord.	2. Replace the cord.
	3. Burned-out motor.	3. Check the cost of a replacement motor first; it may be less expensive to buy a new electric can opener.
Motor hums, but can opener fails to operate	1. Broken or damaged gear.	1. Replace the broken gear with a duplicate made for your brand of can opener. Check the unit for bearing wear.
Can opener generates excessive noise	1. Broken or damaged gear.	1. Replace the broken gear with a duplicate made for your brand of can opener. Check the unit for bearing wear.

You are unlikely to encounter any motor difficulty with your electric can opener. Nevertheless, you should lubricate the bearings if they bind. In addition, you should inspect the gear mechanism regularly. Sometimes, a worn bearing allows the gears to become misaligned, with gear breakage being the end result. If you find a stripped or chipped gear, always check to be sure that the bearings are in good condition. Then, install new gears and align them properly.

The most common maintenance you must perform on an electric can opener is cleaning. Remove the cutter blade or wheel, and inspect it for chips as well as food residue. If you find that the cutter blade is chipped or dull, replace it. Install the new blade with the beveled side facing the inside to prevent binding. If the cutter blade is merely dirty, soak it in a solution of hot water and dishwashing detergent for several hours, and then brush it thoroughly with an old toothbrush and rinse.

ELECTRIC KNIVES

Electric knives can be battery powered (cordless), or they can operate from a household receptacle. Either a universal motor or a miniature DC motor provides the power. A reduction gear is attached to the motor to reduce its speed and to increase its power. Usually, the motor has a worm gear cut into the end of the rotor shaft to turn the pinion gear. As the worm gear drives the pinion, the off-center blade attachment converts the rotary motion of the pinion into the back-and-forth motion of the blades.

The blade itself is divided into two pieces, and the sockets are attached to the pinion in such a way that as one blade is pulling back, the other is

Ronson's Carve 'N' Slice can cut most foods easily.

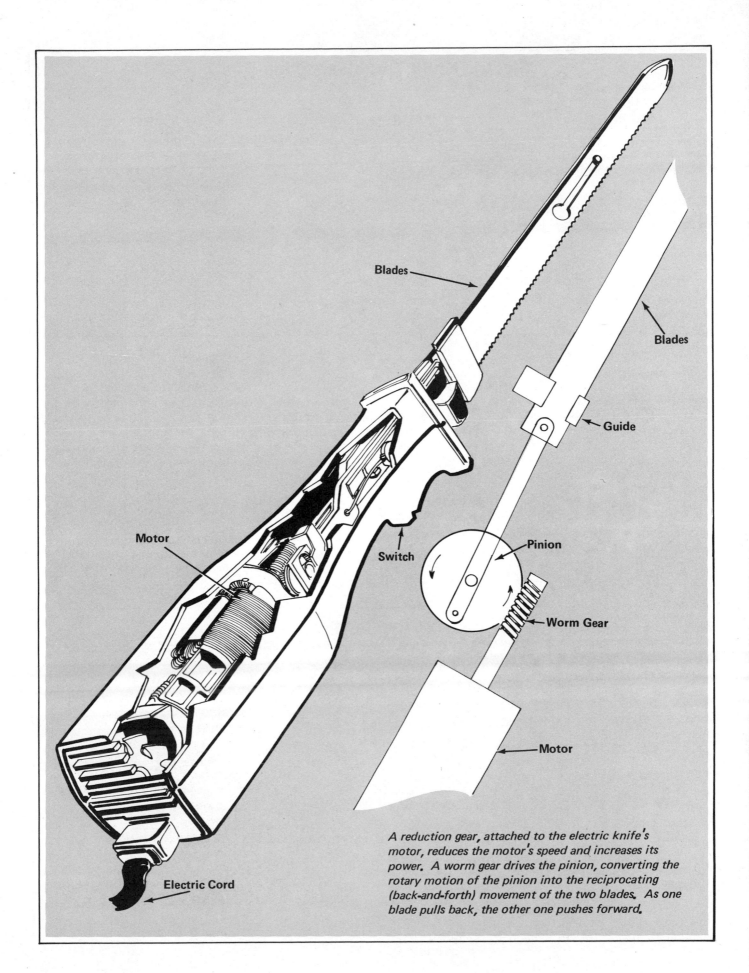

Blades

Blades

Guide

Motor

Switch

Pinion

Worm Gear

Motor

Electric Cord

A reduction gear, attached to the electric knife's motor, reduces the motor's speed and increases its power. A worm gear drives the pinion, converting the rotary motion of the pinion into the reciprocating (back-and-forth) movement of the two blades. As one blade pulls back, the other one pushes forward.

Electric Knife Troubleshooting Chart

Caution: *Unplug appliance before inspecting or repairing. Do not reconnect power until job is completed or while any wiring connections are exposed.*

PROBLEMS	CAUSES	REPAIRS
Electric knife fails to run	1. No voltage from receptacle.	1. Check the condition of the receptacle with a table lamp, and make necessary repairs.
	2. Worn brushes in knife motor.	2. Inspect the brushes and replace them if they are less than 1/4-inch long.
	3. Poor contact between charger base and knife (cordless models).	3. Clean the contact.
Knife does not cut properly	1. Damaged blades.	1. Replace blade assembly.
Motor runs, but blades fail to move	1. Damaged gears or drive unit.	1. Inspect the drive system, and repair it if necessary.

moving forward. This action allows the serrated blades to cut through most meats easily.

Electric knives often suffer wiring connection and cord problems, particularly if the cord is detachable. The charger for a battery-operated knife, usually built into the storage base, must be kept clean in order for the electrical connections to function properly.

Always unplug the knife and remove the blades before you attempt to service one of these appliances. If a blade becomes damaged or misaligned, you have to return the blade to the factory; the blades in your knife must be a matched set.

Motor problems that can arise in an electric knife are those common to all brush-driven motors. You may have to replace the brushes or clean the commutator. Knowing as much as you can about such motors will help you to remedy any faults as they occur.

BLENDERS

The blender is a simple appliance, consisting primarily of a universal motor located in the

Blenders Troubleshooting Chart

Caution: *Unplug appliance before inspecting or repairing. Do not reconnect power until job is completed or while any wiring connections are exposed.*

PROBLEMS	CAUSES	REPAIRS
Blender fails to run	1. No voltage to receptacle.	1. Check the receptacle with a table lamp, and repair if necessary.
	2. Defective switch in blender.	2. Test the switch with a continuity tester, and replace the switch if it is defective.
	3. Worn brushes.	3. Inspect and replace the brushes if they are less than 1/4-inch long.
Cutter unit leaks	1. Defective seal or bearing.	1. Replace the cutter assembly.
Blending or chopping action inadequate	1. Damaged or dull cutter blades.	1. Replace the cutter blade assembly.
	2. Poor coupling between motor base and cutter unit.	2. Inspect the coupling; clean, repair, or replace it as indicated.

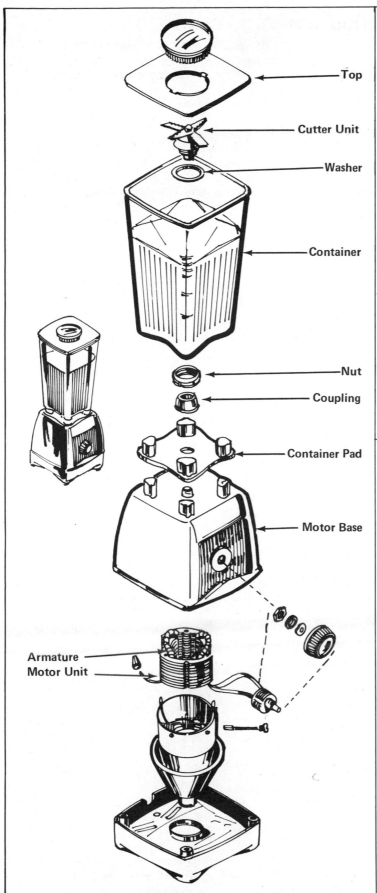

Top

Cutter Unit

Washer

Container

Nut

Coupling

Container Pad

Motor Base

Armature
Motor Unit

Hamilton Beach's System I blender allows you to program a specific blending time at any of the speeds.

Waring's 7-speed blender has a removable blade assembly for easy and efficient cleaning.

base, a food container, and the cutter blades. When you place the container on the motor base, the motor drives the cutter blade assembly through a coupling. The coupling halves in the container and in the base are mated, and they are held in place by the weight of the upper food container.

Unless the container breaks, the only blender problems you are likely to encounter are usually limited to the motor unit and cutters. Since there are a number of taps into the motor field to provide various speeds, look for loose connections in the motor base, and check the condition of the motor brushes. If a coupling slips or breaks, you may be able to bond the coupling back together with a strong — yet pliable — cement. If you cannot fix the broken coupling, then you must replace it. Most couplings are attached to the cutting unit with a threaded nut. If you find such a nut, you can remove the coupling by turning it in the opposite direction from which the motor turns.

If cutter blades become damaged, replace them by loosening the coupling nut — the same way you would to remove the coupling — and install new cutter blades. You should also check the condition of the bearing surface in the cutter assembly, and look for defective seals that would cause leakage into the motor unit. If you discover seals that leak, replace them or consider replacing the entire cutter unit.

ELECTRIC FANS

An electric fan is probably the simplest motorized appliance that exists. It consists of a blade attached to a motor (usually a shaded-pole, though some larger fans use a split-phase motor), with a guard or cage around the blade to prevent injury. The fan blade is shaped to move as much air as possible when it revolves.

Electric fans can be used for many purposes. Although they can be used to good advantage to remove warm air from the home, window fans are often used improperly. During daylight hours, for example, air outside the home becomes superheated by the sun. If you try to move this air inside, it serves only to raise the temperature inside the room. At night or during the evening, however, the fan can bring in the cool outside air and lower the inside temperature. Therefore, you should never operate a window fan during the day when the outside air is hot. Use the fan only when the sun goes down to pull the outside air into your home.

You can also use your electric fan as an exhaust fan for blowing air out of the window in which the fan is mounted. The exhaust action brings fresh air into your home to replace what has been pushed out. If you open windows at the opposite end from where the fan is located, moreover, you allow

Electric Fans Troubleshooting Chart

Caution: Unplug appliance before inspecting or repairing. Do not reconnect power until job is completed or while any wiring connections are exposed.

PROBLEMS	CAUSES	REPAIRS
Fan fails to operate	1. No voltage to receptacle.	1. Test the receptacle with table lamp; repair if required.
	2. Defective fan switch.	2. Test the switch with a continuity tester; replace the switch if it is defective.
	3. Defective fan motor.	3. Test the motor and replace it if it is defective.
Fan makes noise or vibrates	1. Fan blade is out of balance.	1. Place the blade on a flat surface and measure from the surface to the tip of each blade. Straighten the blades if necessary. If damage or misalignment is severe, replace the blade.
	2. Dirty blade.	2. Clean the blade and then reinstall it.
Fan fails to move air properly	1. Damaged fan blade.	1. Inspect the blade and repair it if necessary.
	2. Belts slip.	2. Adjust the belts by loosening the motor mounting brackets. The belts should have 1/2-inch of play when depressed between pulleys.

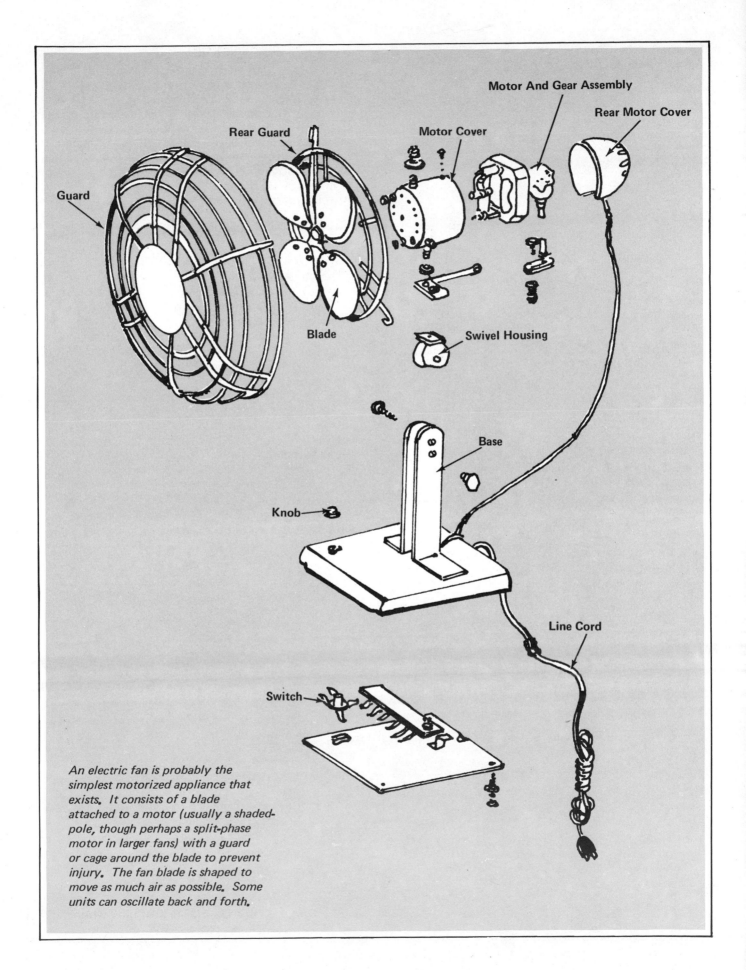

Guard

Rear Guard

Motor Cover

Motor And Gear Assembly

Rear Motor Cover

Blade

Swivel Housing

Base

Knob

Switch

Line Cord

An electric fan is probably the simplest motorized appliance that exists. It consists of a blade attached to a motor (usually a shaded-pole, though perhaps a split-phase motor in larger fans) with a guard or cage around the blade to prevent injury. The fan blade is shaped to move as much air as possible. Some units can oscillate back and forth.

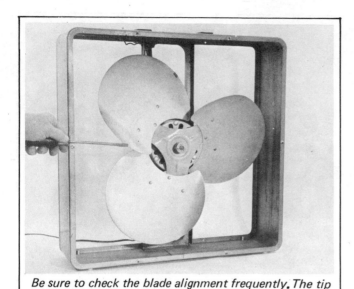

Be sure to check the blade alignment frequently. The tip of each blade should just touch the end of the screwdriver as you rotate the fan blade.

operational adjustment, be sure to unplug the fan. To check blade alignment, place the blade on a table and use a ruler to measure the distance from the table to each blade tip. The tips of all the blades should be the same height from the table. Blades that are bent or warped badly will cause vibration — and if the problem is severe, you should replace the blade unit. Keep the openings in the motor housing free of lint and dust, and lubricate your portable electric fan twice yearly (or as recommended by the manufacturer).

VACUUM CLEANERS

Vacuum cleaners exist in two distinct forms. In the canister vacuum, a universal motor powers a large fan (or impeller) which pushes air out of the vacuum. Often, several impellers are stacked to create better efficiency. As air goes out, other air is drawn in to replace that which has been evacuated. The canister is designed in such a way that the new air comes from the inlet to which you plug the vacuum hose.

You attach the special cleaning tools at the opposite end of the hose. These tools include brushes or wands which help to dislodge dust and lint from floors, walls, crevices, etc. The dust and lint then pass through the wand (the stiff metal or plastic tube attached to the end of the hose), through the flexible hose, and into the vacuum canister itself. Here, a special bag acts as a filter. The bag is designed so that air can pass through, but not even the tiniest particles of lint, dust, and dirt can escape

the fresh air to circulate throughout the entire area.

Some fans have a small gear train attached to the end of the rotor that is opposite the fan blade itself. This gear train turns a linkage that is attached to the base, thereby causing the head of the fan to oscillate back and forth. You can usually control the degree of the fan's oscillation by turning an adjustment nut.

Before you attempt any service procedure or

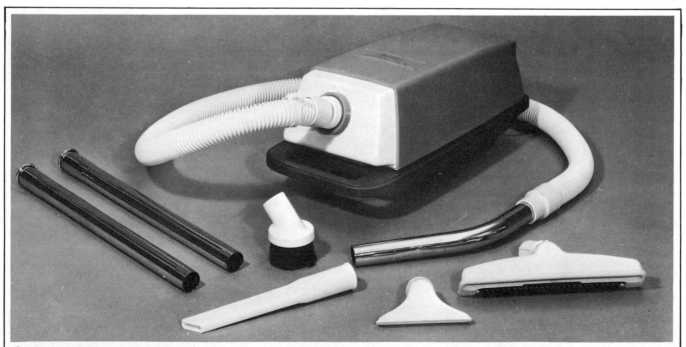

Canister vacs, like the Sears Model 2128, come with wands and tools for cleaning hard-to-reach locations.

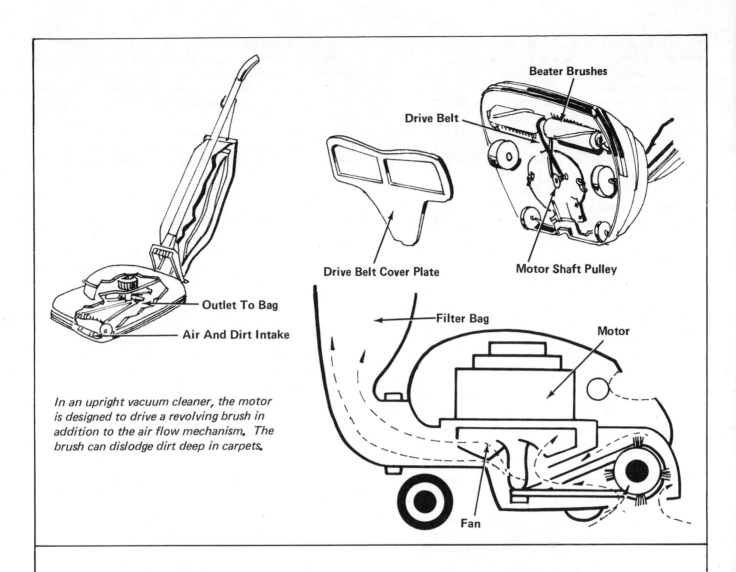

Beater Brushes

Drive Belt

Drive Belt Cover Plate

Motor Shaft Pulley

Outlet To Bag

Air And Dirt Intake

Filter Bag

Motor

Fan

In an upright vacuum cleaner, the motor is designed to drive a revolving brush in addition to the air flow mechanism. The brush can dislodge dirt deep in carpets.

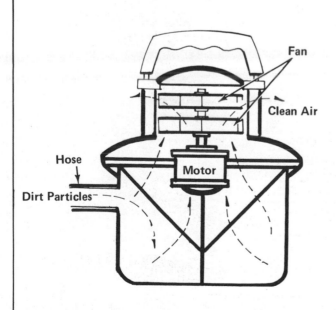

Fan

Clean Air

Hose

Motor

Dirt Particles

In the canister vacuum cleaner, a universal motor powers a large fan (or impeller) which pushes air out of the vacuum. As air goes out, new air is drawn in from the inlet to which you plug the vacuum hose.

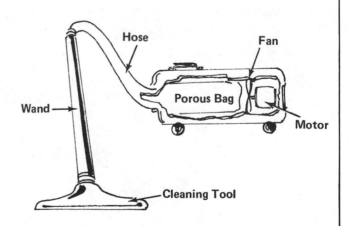

Hose

Fan

Wand

Porous Bag

Motor

Cleaning Tool

— these particles are, instead, trapped and held within the bag.

Since the air must also pass across the impellers and across the motor windings — cooling them as it leaves the vacuum — another protective filter is provided at the motor. If this filter becomes clogged, dust and dirt can damage the motor assembly (particularly the bearings).

In the upright vacuum, the motor is designed to drive a revolving brush in addition to the air flow mechanism. The upright is superior to the canister for carpet cleaning because its revolving brush can dislodge deep dirt near the base of the nap. The machine's suction then carries the soil-laden air into a porous bag which is usually suspended from the handle on most upright models.

Several of the newer and more expensive canisters also have an accessory attachment to give them the versatility of the upright vacuum. They come with a motorized revolving brush (the motor is self-contained within the accessory itself) which you can put on the canister much as you would any ordinary carpet attachment. The accessory device combines the strong suction from the canister with the attachment's revolving brush action to provide excellent cleaning of deep-down carpet fibers. Since the suction is independent of the attachment, the only maintenance problems that the revolving brush accessory could offer would involve bearing, motor, and belt replacements within the unit itself.

One of the most common problems to strike any vacuum cleaner is a lack of suction. If you notice such a lack, turn off the vacuum and remove the hose. Now, turn the vacuum back on and place your hand across the air inlet to see whether suction exists there. If it does, then the blockage problem is in the hose. Nails, toothpicks, etc., can become wedged diagonally in the hose and prevent your vacuum cleaner from operating as it should. Most hose blockage problems are easy to remedy. Remove the hose from the vacuum and take it outside. Push an ordinary garden hose (one that is of a smaller diameter, of course) through the vacuum hose. The garden hose should dislodge any foreign objects within the vacuum hose.

If there is no suction at the inlet, then the problem is within the vacuum itself. Check to be sure that the bag is empty. A full bag prevents air from passing, with the result, of course, that no suction can be produced. Empty (or change) the bag regularly.

Check the protective motor filter whenever you empty the bag. Since many of these filters are washable, you should have no difficulty in keeping it

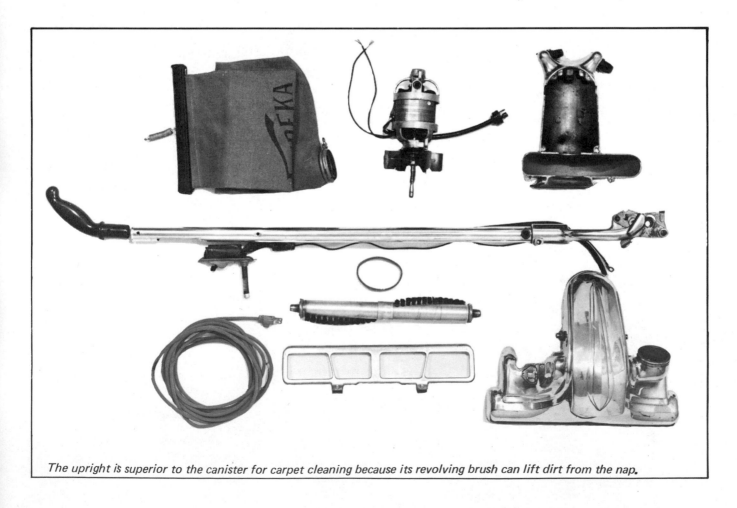

The upright is superior to the canister for carpet cleaning because its revolving brush can lift dirt from the nap.

clean. A filter that becomes severely blocked can cause a reduction in suction and can even produce motor damage. If the filter begins to tear, however, replace it; some manufacturers even recommend that you replace the filter annually whether it is torn or not. Never operate a vacuum cleaner that does not have its protective motor filter in place.

FLOOR POLISHERS

Floor polishers utilize a universal motor to drive two brushes which revolve in opposite directions. Within the floor polisher's base housing, both ends of the motor's rotor are attached to a gear box (or else a worm gear is cut into the rotor shaft itself). In either case, the motor's output drives a pinion gear to which the brushes are connected. This arrangement provides the speed reduction necessary to render substantial power and proper brush rotation. The wax dispenser operates via an orifice which you can open and close to allow the liquid to flow through a tube and into the area near the polishing brushes at the base of the appliance.

Problems that may afflict the motor of a floor polisher are common to most other appliances with universal motors. You must be extremely careful with all floor polisher dispensers. All hoses and fittings must be in good shape and installed properly. Leakage of the waxy liquid within the cabinet could damage the motor. In addition, water or cleaning-agent seepage into the housing could remove the lubrication and damage the bearings, and might even damage some of the electrical insulation.

Most floor polisher problems are caused by improper use of accessory attachments. Since each accessory is designed to operate at a certain speed, the floor polisher is designed to provide these speeds through tapped field windings in the universal motor. You must use only the recommended speeds for the particular attachments or polishing pads that you own. An improper speed can lead to motor failure. In some cases, the type of flooring you have affects the speed setting recommended by the manufacturer.

Always unplug the polisher before you proceed with any sort of servicing. The liquid dispenser, which is simply a container with a plug blocking an outlet orifice, should be flushed thoroughly with clean water after every use. When reassembling a polisher after inspection and repair, be sure that all gaskets and seals are in place to prevent any fluid leakage into the motor housing. Moreover, make certain that the gear box in the motor housing is properly lubricated at all times.

Vacuum Cleaners Troubleshooting Chart

Caution: Unplug appliance before inspecting or repairing. Do not reconnect power until job is completed or while any wiring connections are exposed.

PROBLEMS	CAUSES	REPAIRS
Motor will not run	1. No voltage reaching vacuum. 2. Damaged power cord. 3. Worn motor brushes. 4. Bad on-off switch. 5. Damaged motor.	1. Check the condition of the receptacle with a table lamp. 2. Replace the cord. 3. Replace the brushes. 4. Replace the switch. 5. Repair if possible; replace if necessary.
Vacuum cleaner emits shock when motor is started	1. Wire has come loose and is grounded against unit's case or the motor windings are grounded.	1. Take the vacuum cleaner to a professional service technician; do not use the appliance again until the fault ground is found and repaired.
Upright vac is hard to push	1. Carpet height adjustment set too low (too close to floor). 2. Worn-out brushes. 3. Brush spindles need lubrication.	1. Raise the carpet height adjustment. 2. Replace the brushes. 3. Follow the diagram in your owner's manual for proper lubrication.
Lack of suction	1. Foreign object in the base or attachments. 2. The bag or protective filter is full.	1. Check the hose and clear any blockage. 2. Replace or empty the bag; replace the filter.

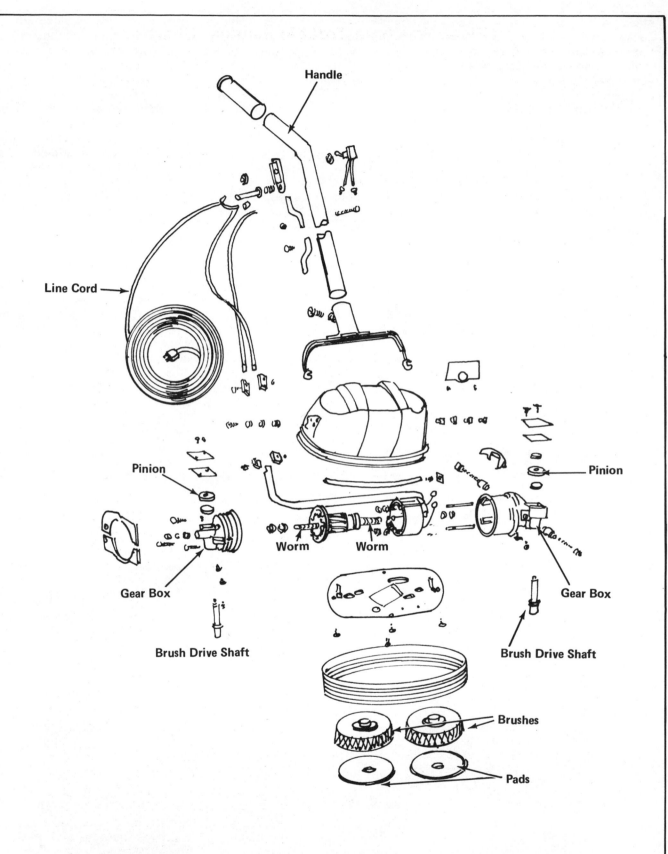

Handle

Line Cord

Pinion

Pinion

Gear Box

Worm

Worm

Gear Box

Brush Drive Shaft

Brush Drive Shaft

Brushes

Pads

Floor polishers utilize a universal motor to drive two brushes in opposite directions. Within the floor polisher's base housing, both ends of a rotor are attached to a gear box, and the motor's output drives a pinion gear to which the brushes are connected.

Floor Polishers Troubleshooting Chart

Caution: Unplug appliance before inspecting or repairing. Do not reconnect power until job is completed or while any wiring connections are exposed.

PROBLEMS	CAUSES	REPAIRS
Polisher fails to run	1. No voltage to receptacle.	1. Check the receptacle with a table lamp and repair if necessary.
	2. Defective cord or plug.	2. Check the cord and plug; replace any defective parts.
	3. Defective switch.	3. Check the switch with a continuity tester, and replace if necessary.
Brushes do not revolve	1. Damaged gears.	1. Inspect the gears and replace any damaged ones.
Dispenser does not work	1. Clog in dispenser or line.	1. Flush the unit with clear hot water.
Polisher emits electrical shocks	1. Grounded component or wiring.	1. Locate the ground fault with a continuity tester, and either repair the fault or replace the polisher.

HUMIDIFIERS

The humidifier is a very important appliance. During the winter, the warm furnace air circulating through the house tends to dry out both your furnishings as well as the structure of the house itself. To maintain the proper water balance in the air, you must add moisture artificially. That is where the humidifier comes in.

You should be able to find a humidifier to satisfy the needs of practically any home. Portable humidifiers, designed to serve one portion of your

McGraw Edison Model 39 is a drum-type evaporative unit.

Presto 801 distributes humidity through top and sides.

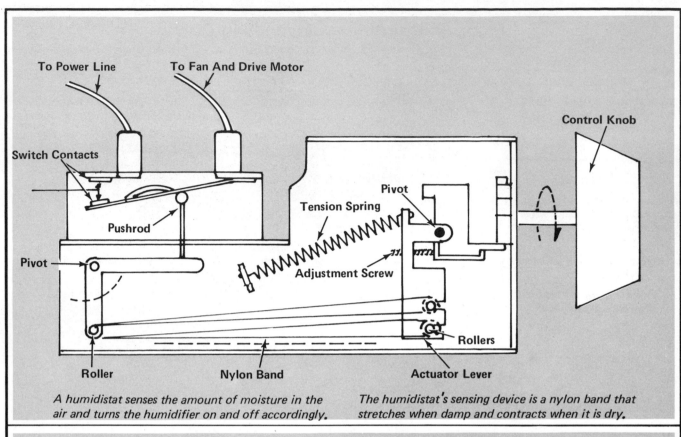

To Power Line · To Fan And Drive Motor · Control Knob · Switch Contacts · Pivot · Tension Spring · Pivot · Pushrod · Adjustment Screw · Roller · Rollers · Pivot · Roller · Nylon Band · Actuator Lever

A humidistat senses the amount of moisture in the air and turns the humidifier on and off accordingly.

The humidistat's sensing device is a nylon band that stretches when damp and contracts when it is dry.

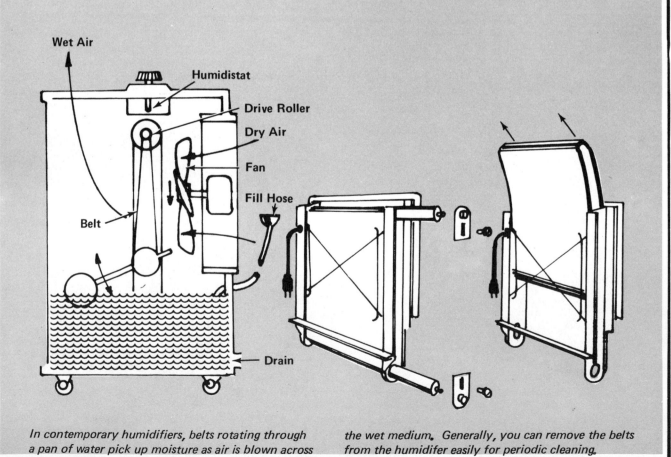

Wet Air · Humidistat · Drive Roller · Dry Air · Fan · Fill Hose · Belt · Drain

In contemporary humidifiers, belts rotating through a pan of water pick up moisture as air is blown across

the wet medium. Generally, you can remove the belts from the humidifer easily for periodic cleaning.

home, are usually units that have their own motor and blower. Although most models must be refilled with water frequently, some portable humidifiers can be permanently connected to the water supply, eliminating the need for manual filling. Still other humidifiers are designed to be installed in the warm air system of the furnace. Generally, such units connect on the supply plenum (the large box on the furnace from which the supply ducts to the rooms originate), and the moisture gets picked up and carried with the warm air to each room of the house.

There are several ways to get moisture into the air. One is the evaporative method. In its simplest form, the evaporative humidifier consists simply of mineral-based absorbent plates that are placed in a pan of water. The warm air which circulates around these plates absorbs some of the moisture, helping to replenish the water content of the heated air.

The old-fashioned evaporative humidifier is generally considered quite insufficient, however. Today, most humidifiers possess porous foam materials to act as the media or evaporative surface. Water pumped across this media material and air forced through it allow the modern humidifier to generate much more moisture than the older units ever could. In some contemporary models, belts rotating through a pan of water pick up moisture constantly as air is blown across the wet medium material. The humidifier may have its own blower or

Room-type humidifiers have their own blowers, while other units use furnace air to circulate moisture.

it may use the air from the furnace blower to circulate the moisture.

Atomizing humidifiers have also become quite popular. In some atomizing units, a disk that

Humidifiers Troubleshooting Chart

Caution: Unplug the humidifier or disconnect the electrical power before inspecting or repairing. Do not reconnect power until the job is completed or while any wiring connections are exposed. If humidifier is attached to the furnace, turn off the furnace before inspecting or servicing the humidifier.

PROBLEMS	CAUSES	REPAIRS
Humidifier fails to run	1. No power to humidifier.	1. Check the receptacle with a table lamp for a portable humidifier; check the fuse for a built-in humidifier.
	2. Motor binding.	2. Check for mineral deposits on media and/or motor bearings.
Insufficient humidity	1. Water supply shut off.	1. Check the water supply, and make sure that the valves are turned on.
	2. Humidistat set too low.	2. Raise the humidistat setting.
	3. Media pad clogged.	3. Remove the media pad and clean or replace it.
Humidifier overflows	1. Water-inlet float valve stuck.	1. Clean or repair the valve. Look for foreign matter on the valve seat.
	2. Mineral buildup on case causing siphoning.	2. Clean the water container of mineral deposits.

In furnace-mounted humidifiers, a water line leads into the humidifier pan from a main water pipe. The forced air from the furnace picks up the moisture and then circulates moistened air through your home.

VAPORIZING HUMIDIFIER

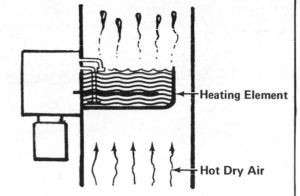

Heating Element

Hot Dry Air

EVAPORATIVE HUMIDIFIER

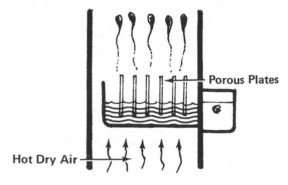

Porous Plates

Hot Dry Air

ATOMIZING HUMIDIFIER

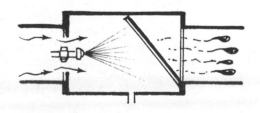

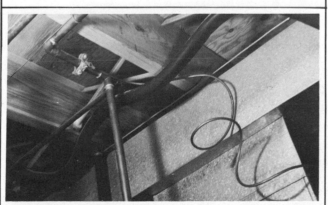

Although most humidifiers must be refilled with water, others can be connected to your home's water supply.

revolves at high speeds picks up water from a pump and then — by centrifugal force — slings the water off in a fine mist. The mist, of course, is absorbed into the warm air supply leading into each room. Another version of the atomizing humidifier utilizes water pressure to provide the fine mist. Water passes first through an electrically operated valve and then through a special nozzle where it enters the warm air system almost like a cloud of vapor.

High-capacity humidifiers like the atomizing units must have some sort of control to prevent their oversaturating your home. A humidistat, often mounted in a return air duct, senses the amount of moisture in the air and turns the humidifier on and off to maintain the proper moisture level. Such humidistats are usually adjustable. If yours is, set it at around 40 percent relative humidity, the ideal moisture level within the home. Setting it at levels considerably higher than 40 percent can cause condensation problems.

A humidifier requires regular maintenance during the winter season. Naturally, you must make certain that the humidifier is turned off before attempting any service or maintenance. If the manufacturer recommends oiling the motor, use only a few drops at the beginning of each winter; the few drops should be enough lubrication for the season. If you have an atomizing humidifier, check the filter screen at least once during the season. Clean the screen thoroughly before placing it back into service. Clean the pan and/or media belt of an evaporative humidifier regularly. Soak the pan in a solution of white vinegar and water, and then scrape away minerals. You can clean media belts in the same manner, but never scrape them. Rinse the belt well and drain it; you must handle the belt carefully, particularly when it is dry. If a media belt becomes caked and cannot be cleaned thoroughly, it should be replaced.

Never connect the humidifier to a soft water line. A water softener replaces calcium salts with sodium salts, a process which can be detrimental to a humidifier's quality of operation. Connect a humidifier only to an untreated water line.

ELECTRIC TOOTHBRUSHES

There are two types of electric toothbrushes: some units have a small battery as the power source, while others utilize a miniature 115-volt motor in the appliance handle. Battery-driven models have a recharging device built into the unit's storage base; you must, of course, plug the recharging device into a receptacle in order to charge the toothbrush unit's batteries.

The motor in either type of electric toothbrush turns a pinion which, in turn, drives a bevel gear. An eccentric linkage attached to the bevel gear generates the brush's movement itself. For the most part, electric toothbrushes are not repairable, and there is little in the way of preventive maintenance that you can do. Naturally, you should always avoid

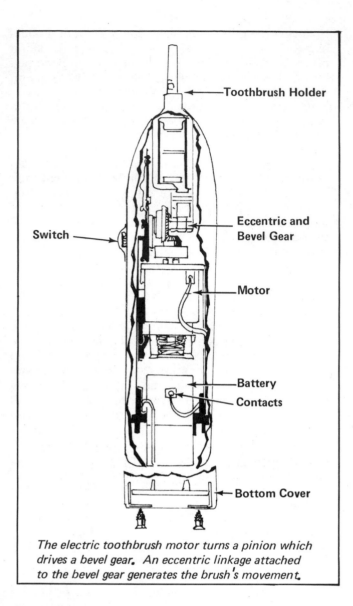

The electric toothbrush motor turns a pinion which drives a bevel gear. An eccentric linkage attached to the bevel gear generates the brush's movement.

do to repair or maintain the unit. If your electric toothbrush fails to operate, check the connection between the charger base and the brush. If the connection is corroded, the batteries cannot be recharged and the brush stops working. You can try to clean the connection — with the unit disconnected, of course — but you may have to replace your electric toothbrush if the connection is corroded beyond simple repair.

ELECTRIC SHAVERS

Electric shavers can be driven by a vibrator motor, a tiny universal motor, or a miniature DC motor. Some models have rotary blades which are driven from the motor unit itself, while others utilize a vibrator device to provide the oscillating motion which drives the blades. Still another arrangement finds an eccentric attached to the pinion of the motor. In any case, the idea in all electric shavers is to move a blade that accomplishes the cutting action.

There are two sets of blades in an electric shaver. In most cases, the outer blade set is stationary. The whisker penetrates through an opening or slot in the outer blade set, and then the inner blade set — which is revolving or oscillating — can shear the whisker off by moving back past the opening.

The cordless type shavers operate from nicad batteries within the shaver housing. Generally, you can recharge the batteries by merely inserting the shaver into a charging unit in the base of the shaver's storage case. Nearly all types of rechargeable shavers use miniature DC motors to power the cutting action.

Follow the manufacturer's instructions for cleaning the shaver, and clean it regularly. If you keep your shaver clean, you should encounter little trouble — unless you happen to drop the appliance or abuse it in some other way. The heads of most shavers are replaceable, but you must replace both sets of blades simultaneously; they are a matched pair. Brushes and other internal parts of the shaver's motor unit can be hard to find; in large cities, check with distributors for the parts you need. Otherwise, you must return the razor to the factory for repair.

immersing the toothbrush in water, and you must handle it carefully to eliminate the possibility of damage brought about by dropping the appliance.

Since the housing of an electric toothbrush is sealed, however, there is little more that you can

Electric Toothbrush Troubleshooting Chart

Caution: Unplug appliance before inspecting or repairing. Do not reconnect power until job is completed or while any wiring connections are exposed.

PROBLEMS	CAUSES	REPAIRS
Portable unit fails to hold charge	1. Defective batteries or charger.	1. Replace the entire unit.
	2. Batteries run down immediately after charging.	2. Poor contact between the toothbrush and base; clean the contact and retest.

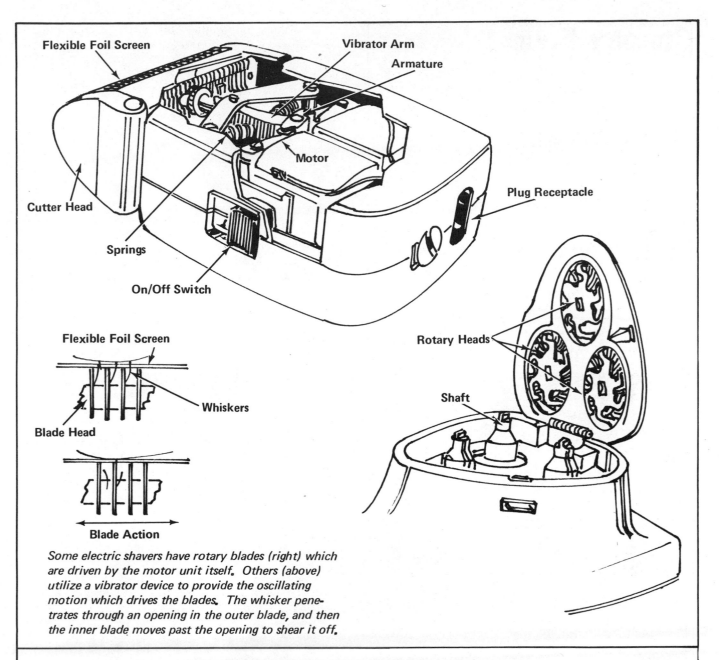

Some electric shavers have rotary blades (right) which are driven by the motor unit itself. Others (above) utilize a vibrator device to provide the oscillating motion which drives the blades. The whisker penetrates through an opening in the outer blade, and then the inner blade moves past the opening to shear it off.

Electric Shavers Troubleshooting Chart

Caution: Unplug appliance before inspecting or repairing. Do not reconnect power until job is completed or while any wiring connections are exposed.

PROBLEMS	CAUSES	REPAIRS
Shaver fails to operate	1. No voltage to the receptacle.	1. Check the receptacle with a table lamp, and repair if necessary.
	2. Poor contact between charger base and shaver (battery or cordless models only).	2. Clean the contacts between the shaver and its charger base.
Shaver does not cut properly	1. Dirty head	1. Clean the heads thoroughly.
	2. Damaged or worn head	2. Replace the head assembly.

Chapter Four

Major Appliances

Major appliances need not saddle you with either major headaches or major repair bills. For the most part, these appliances involve the same components with which you are already familiar from the discussions of heating appliances and motorized small appliances. Therefore, if you know something about motors, solenoids, heating elements, etc., you can perform an enormous number of major and minor repairs yourself and save plenty of money in the process.

Most importantly, however, you can keep your appliances running the way they should merely by following certain simple preventive maintenance procedures regularly. Not only will such maintenance help you derive the benefits of maximum efficiency and performance, but it also will result in a longer and more trouble-free life for your air conditioner, dishwasher, trash compactor, disposer, washer, dryer, water heater, range, and refrigerator.

AIR CONDITIONERS

The air conditioner moves heat from one area to another much like the cooling system in a frostless refrigerator. Inside the unit there is a coil called the evaporator, and it is the component that gets cold. A fan pulls heated air from the room across the evaporator coil, and then pushes the cooled air into the living area. Warm air is constantly being pulled back through the air conditioner unit and across the coil, creating a complete recirculating process. In addition, the air conditioner helps to lower the humidity level in your home, and thereby enhance the comfort of the living area. The moisture in the heat-laden air tends to collect upon the chilled coils of the evaporator, much as condensation does on the outside of a glass of iced tea during summertime.

What happens to the heat? It is carried by the refrigeration system to an exterior coil called the condenser. The condenser, which is hot to the touch, is exposed to the outside air. The circulating outside air absorbs the heat, dispelling it outside your home. Meanwhile, air is continually pulled through louvers in the sides of the cabinet and pushed out through the coils. This process eventually eliminates enough of the hot air in your home to make it comfortable.

The same heat-removal principles apply as much to an automobile's air conditioning system as they do to a centralized home or window unit. In a car, the evaporator (which is located behind the dash) removes the heat and transfers it to the condenser (usually located in front of the car's radiator). In a home central air conditioning system, the condenser and compressor may be remote (located on the roof or as a separate unit somewhere outside the house). The evaporator of a central air conditioning system is placed within the supply duct plenum of the furnace.

The compressor acts as a pump to circulate the refrigerant through the system. Therefore, you can control the temperature in your home with a thermostat which simply turns the compressor on and off to maintain the degree of coolness you desire. In most cases, the system's blowers continue to run even when the compressor is off. Fan motors consume only a small amount of electricity, and they help keep air circulating within the room even when the cooling system itself is not required. Without continual air circulation, the cold air would collect near the floor, a condition known as "stratification" which can be quite uncomfortable.

Many central and window type air conditioners possess a large oil-filled running capacitor to increase the compressor's efficiency and to lower the system's operating costs. Never attempt to

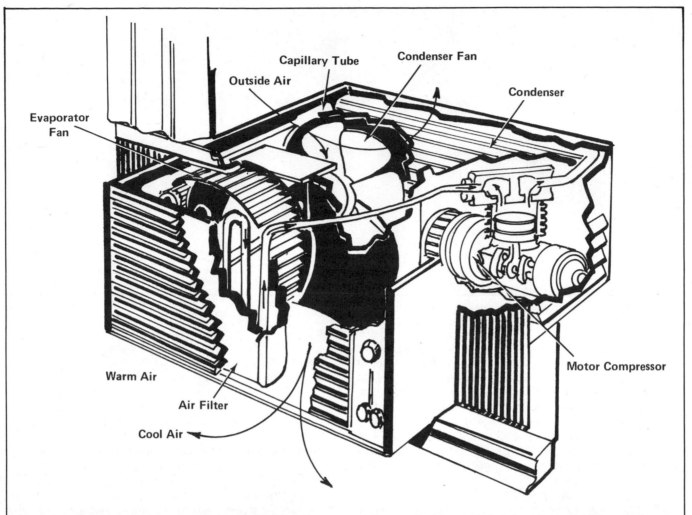

Evaporator Fan

Outside Air

Capillary Tube

Condenser Fan

Condenser

Warm Air

Air Filter

Cool Air

Motor Compressor

A fan pulls heated air from the room across the evaporator, and then pushes the cooled air back into the living area.

Carrier's Weatherette 100 Portable air conditioner comes in 5000 and 8000 BTU capacities for one-room cooling.

handle or test this capacitor without first discharging it with a 20,000-ohm, 2-watt, wire-wound resistor. All in all, capacitor work is a job best left to the professional refrigeration repairmen. The capacitor is a storehouse for electricity, and if you handle it improperly, you can receive a dangerous or even fatal electrical shock. You must, of course, disconnect the air conditioner from the power supply before you perform any sort of maintenance or service upon it.

All air conditioners require regular maintenance, consisting primarily of the cleaning and replacing of filters at specified intervals (once every 30 days is not too often). Dirty filters, as you would expect, reduce the air flow and lower the efficiency of the unit. In severe cases, filters that fail to do their job can even damage the evaporator and the compressor. Therefore, you must clean or change the filters regularly.

Filters made of foam or aluminum are washable; you can flush these filters with a hose from the back side. Some air conditioner manufacturers recommend that you then coat the clean filter fibers with a special adhesive to trap particles as the air passes through the filter. Fiberglass filters, however, cannot be cleaned; you must replace fiberglass filters when they become dirty.

If a filter has been clogged for a long period of time, lint and dirt can work their way through to clog the evaporator coil itself. You can remedy this situation by applying a special cleaning solution or a strong liquid detergent to the coil. Spread the solution on the coil and allow it to soak for a few minutes. Then spray the coil with water, and brush away the residue from the front. Continue to flush the coil until it appears to be free from lint and dirt once again.

The water you use to rinse the evaporator coil will flow out the same drain line that carries off condensate water when the air conditioner is operating. Such water usually flows across the base pan to a sump located at the bottom of the condenser fan blade. This fan blade has a special ring around it (called a "slinger" ring) that rises through the puddle at the bottom of the condenser. The slinger ring helps eliminate dripping — except in the most humid weather — and it also increases the efficiency of the condenser. The condensate water cools the refrigerant in the system more quickly than the air around the condenser ever could.

If the evaporator or condenser fins ever become bent, you can straighten them with a "Fin Comb" — available at a refrigeration supply store. You must take every precaution to keep the air flow to the condenser unimpeded. Never let bushes crowd either the front of the condenser or the air intake louvers at the sides of the cabinet.

Most large window units today have a slide-out chassis, which allows you access to the machine's operating components. Clean the components annually by first vacuuming the parts and then flushing them with clear water. If any algae is

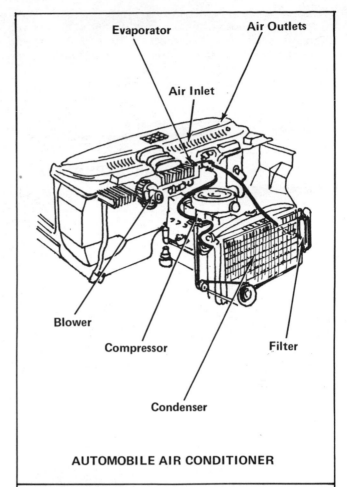

AUTOMOBILE AIR CONDITIONER

Most large window units have a slide-out chassis.

present, add a spoonful of household ammonia to the rinse water to make removal easy. Again, be sure that the unit is unplugged before you remove the access panels or slide out the chassis.

A single double-shaft fan motor, mounted at or near the partition that separates the evaporator (cold) area from the condenser (warm) area, is often used to drive both of the air conditioner's fans. If you find oil ports near the motor's front and rear end housing, apply a few drops of oil to them at the beginning of every summer.

Most air conditioner repairs within the unit's electrical and refrigeration systems should be left to professional service personnel. If you follow the maintenance procedures outlined here, however, you should be able to eliminate the majority of air conditioner problems before they necessitate major repairs and enjoy a more efficiently cooled and comfortable home as well.

Air Conditioner Troubleshooting Chart

Caution: Unplug appliance before inspecting or repairing. Do not reconnect power until job is completed or while any wiring connections are exposed.

PROBLEMS	CAUSES	REPAIRS
Air conditioner does not run	1. Blown fuse or tripped circuit breaker.	1. Replace the fuse with one of the correct rating, or reset the circuit breaker. If the fuse blows or circuit breaker trips again, do not operate the unit. An electrical failure exists that could start a fire. Call an electrician.
	2. Broken or loose power cord.	2. First, spread the prongs of the power cord plug, reinsert it into the wall outlet, and try the unit. If this fails, check the service cord over its entire length for breaks and for a loose connection at the control switch end. Replace a defective cord.
	3. Defective thermostat.	3. Check the thermostat for continuity. Replace any broken wires, and refasten any loose wires.
	4. Defective starter capacitor.	4. Capacitors are storehouses of electricity, and they can be very dangerous to handle even when the air conditioner is disconnected. If the starter capacitor is defective, call in a refrigeration repairman.
Air conditioner does not cool	1. Thermostat not set properly.	1. Set thermostat to a lower temperature to provide more cooling.
	2. Dirty filter.	2. Replace or clean the filter.
	3. Condenser coil dirty.	3. Blow or vacuum the dirt from the condenser with the brush attachment of a vacuum cleaner.
	4. Compressor does not run.	4. Check for a defective thermostat, bad capacitor, an open overload switch, or broken or loose wiring. Finally, examine the compressor itself for defects.
	5. Refrigerant leak.	5. Check the unit's tubes and components for leaks.

PROBLEMS	CAUSES	REPAIRS
	6. Unit too small for load imposed.	6. If unit is undersized, it will not adequately cool a room. Install a larger unit.
	7. Air flow through the condenser or evaporator is blocked.	7. Check for furnishings (drapes, chairs) blocking the evaporator, or shrubs blocking the condenser.
Air conditioner operates, but fan does not.	1. Defective fan switch.	1. Check switch for continuity (broken or loose wires).
	2. Defective fan capacitor.	2. Call in a professional repairman to install a new capacitor.
	3. Defective fan motor winding.	3. Check each winding of the motor for continuity.
Unit switches on and off in short cycles	1. Lack of good contact between the evaporator inlet and the thermostatic expansion valve bulb (automotive systems).	1. Make sure that the evaporator is not blocked by dirt or anything else. The thermostatic expansion valve bulb must be touching the evaporator inlet pipe.
	2. Dirty condenser coil.	2. Blow or vacuum the dirt from the condenser with a vacuum cleaner.
	3. Defective capacitor.	3. If the motor stalls when it gets hot, be sure that the bearings are not binding. If the bearings are in order, the problem is in the capacitor or fan motor; call in a professional.
	4. Defective overload switch.	4. A lack of continuity across the overload switch's terminals indicates the need for a new switch.
	5. Unit restarted too soon after being stopped.	5. An air conditioner that is turned on too soon after it was stopped may cause a blown fuse or short cycling. Allow at least five minutes of idle time before restarting a unit that was halted.

AUTOMATIC DISHWASHERS

The automatic dishwasher operates by forcing a high-velocity stream of hot water, mixed with a detergent solution, against dirty dishes. This jet action combined with the high water temperature provide a cleaning action that both scrubs the dishes and eliminates bacteria. The dishwasher then drains the dirty water away, rinses the dishes with fresh hot water, and dries the dishes with hot air.

Like most automatic appliances, the dishwasher is controlled by a timer. The timer is a clock-actuated switch which actually contains a number of switching contacts that can energize different cycles. The clock motor begins to run as soon as you start the machine, and it continues to run until the end of the wash cycle. At that point, a contact opens and breaks the circuit to the timer motor.

Some dishwasher functions are controlled by small electromagnetic devices called solenoids. Solenoids are coils of wire that concentrate the magnetic force surrounding any wire which has current flowing through it. When energized by the timer, a solenoid attracts a pole or armature; this

Stack dishes with some space around them. The soiled sides of cups in the top rack should face the center.

The dishwasher timer is a clock-actuated switch that begins to run as soon as you start the machine.

movement in turn, carries out some mechanical work. In the dishwasher, for example, a solenoid located in a water valve allows water to flow into the machine; the solenoid opens the valve in much the same way that you would open a faucet. When the timer contacts to the solenoid circuit open, current ceases to flow, and the solenoid then shuts the water off.

In most dishwashers, the precise volume of water necessary for efficient operation is controlled by a small regulator in the water valve known as a flow washer. This regulator reduces flow within the line to approximately 20 pounds per square inch,

much lower than the pressure found in most city water mains. Since the flow washer controls the water pressure and the timer controls the length of time that the water inlet is open, dishwasher designers can engineer machines that utilize a specific quantity of water every time they are operated.

Dishwashers use only hot water. Ideally, the water temperature should be between 140 and 150 degrees for proper cleaning of your dishes. If the temperature is less than 140 degrees, the dishwashing detergent cannot dissolve properly and certain greases cannot emulsify entirely. The result, of course, is poor cleaning performance. Consequently, the water temperature is one of the first things that you should check if your dishwasher ever fails to clean properly. You can use a candy or a meat thermometer in the dishwasher to measure the water temperature.

Always measure the water temperature during the second wash cycle. If the water temperature in your dishwasher is too low, then raise the thermostat setting on your water heater. The dishwasher heating element cannot compensate for an insufficiently heated water supply; the element's main responsibility is to maintain the water temperature during normal wash periods. If there were no heating element, the spraying action of the water against the cool sides of the cabinet could lower the water temperature substantially during the course of a single wash period.

Most dishwashers have detergent dispensers that permit the cleaning agent to enter the water at the proper time. Since there are usually two wash cycles, each must have its own charge of detergent. Therefore, one side of the filled dispenser is usually open, while the other is latched shut. When the dishwashing cycle begins, the hot water flushes the detergent from the open container; after the second wash cycle begins, a solenoid (or bimetal strip) unlatches the second compartment, allowing the second charge of detergent to be discharged into the water.

After its wash cycle, the dishwasher goes through several rinse periods to remove any remaining detergent or food particles. In addition, some dishwashers provide two other actions during the final rinse period: one is a sanitizing treatment, and the other reduces spotting.

The sanitizing feature utilizes an electric heating element to raise the water temperature to at least 150 degrees to reduce the bacteria count. The sanitizing cycle turns the timer motor off and allows the heating element to remain on until a bimetal thermostat — which senses the water temperature — closes, turning the timer motor on again. Since it takes about one minute to raise the dishwasher's water temperature one degree, it could take around 30 minutes to heat the water temperature up to the level required by the sanitizing cycle, if your home's hot water temperature is low (around 120 degrees, for instance). This is another good reason to be sure that your hot water temperature is at least 145 degrees.

The second final rinse feature on many dishwashers releases rinse additives from a special dispenser. The dispenser introduces a few drops of a wetting agent into the final rinse water, and the wetting agent allows the water to drain off the dishes without spotting during the drying cycle. Wetting agents are available in solid form for machines that lack a special dispenser.

During the drying cycle, the dishwasher's electric element is energized, heating the air which dries the dishes. Some dishwashers have a small fan which circulates the warmed air through the machine, speeding up the drying process. At the end of the cycle, you should open the compartment door and allow the dishwasher to stand for a few minutes. This allows the condensation to leave the dishes.

There are two basic causes of poor cleaning in automatic dishwashers, and neither has anything to do with the machine itself: low water temperature and defective detergent. Dishwasher detergent ages quickly and has a short shelf life. That is the reason most dishwashing detergents come in rather small packages compared to those that contain laundry detergents. Check your dishwasher detergent regularly by pouring a small amount of it into hot water, stirring, and then allowing it to settle for a few minutes. If a gritty residue remains, you know that your dishwashing detergent is too old to provide good cleaning results. Detergent that is caked should also be thrown away.

Although it is unnecessary to pre-rinse dishes before putting them in the dishwasher, you should brush away bones, olive pits, and other hard foreign objects as well as solid food particles. If a foreign object does get into the pump, however, you may be able to remove it. Turn off the power to the dishwasher, and inspect the area under the basket around the pump inlet. If you cannot find or remove the foreign object, you may have to disassemble the pump. Should you ever hear the pump make a sharp loud grinding noise, turn the machine off immediately and remove the foreign object. Otherwise, damage to the pump — and even to the motor — can occur.

Most dishwashers have a float switch to shut off the water supply if too much water enters the machine. The float is usually located just inside the tank in one of the front corners. If the water ever fails to enter your dishwasher, check the float; it can get jammed by a dish or utensil. If the float is not the problem, check the filter screen in the inlet valve where the water line is attached. Clean the residue from the filter screen and replace it.

If your dishwasher leaks, you should have professional service personnel repair it immediately. The strong detergents and hot water can damage the finish on your flooring and loosen the cement that bonds the tile or linoleum to your floor. Try to locate the general location of the leak, but be sure to turn the power off before you start inspecting a leaking dishwasher.

Dishwashers Troubleshooting Chart

Caution: Unplug appliance before inspecting or repairing. Do not reconnect power until job is completed or while any wiring connections are exposed.

PROBLEMS	CAUSES	REPAIRS
Detergent dispenser cover stays closed	1. Detergent has hardened from being left in dispenser too long or placed into a wet dispenser.	1. Scrape out the hardened detergent and add fresh. The dispenser should be dry when you add detergent.
	2. Dishes or utensils blocking dispenser cover.	2. Position the dishes and utensils so that they do not block the dispenser cover.
	3. Calcium deposits on lid or on shaft.	3. Remove any calcium deposits from around the dispenser mechanism by cleaning with vinegar.
	4. Defective detergent dispenser solenoid valve.	4. Test the solenoid valve with a continuity tester. Replace if defective.
	5. Defective timer.	5. Advance the timer to the position in which the detergent dispenser cover should open. If the cover fails to open, the timer is probably defective. Replace it.

PROBLEMS	CAUSES	REPAIRS
Spotting or film on dishware	1. Dishes stacked improperly.	1. Stack the dishes with some space around them. Avoid clutter. The soiled sides of cups in the top rack should face toward the center of the rack.
	2. Insufficient detergent.	2. Use as much detergent as specified in the instruction book.
	3. Dishes not scraped adequately.	3. All large particles and "clinging" foods such as spinach, broccoli, etc., must be scraped.
	4. Water is too cool.	4. Check the temperature of your home's hot water. It must be at least 140 degrees F.
	5. Water is too hard.	4. Use a rinsing additive.
Specks on dishes	1. Food particles.	1. Clean the filter screen; stack dishes properly; use the proper amount of detergent; see to it that the wash arm's rotation is not blocked by a utensil or dish; and make sure wash arm holes are not clogged by food particles.
	2. Detergent is spoiled.	2. Discard old detergent; if detergent is fresh, do not let it stand in dispenser — add it just before washing.
Dishwasher fails to fill	1. Shut-off water valve partially or fully closed.	1. Check the shut-off valve on the line leading to the dishwasher; open it fully.
	2. Water pressure is too low.	2. Water pressure must be at least 15 pounds per square inch; call your local water company.
	3. Clogged water-inlet screen or damaged water valve.	3. Most water valves are equipped with screens to trap deposits. Disassemble and clean the screen. If the parts are heavily calcified, replace the entire water-inlet valve assembly.
	4. Defective water-valve solenoid.	4. Check the solenoid with a continuity tester. Replace the solenoid if it is open.
	5. Faulty float switch.	5. Some dishwashers are equipped with a float switch in the tub that controls the water valve. Test the float by picking up the float with your finger and letting it drop. You should hear a "click," and the float arm should fall squarely on the float switch. If it does not, replace the float assembly.

PROBLEMS	CAUSES	REPAIRS
Dishwasher leaks	1. Loose or worn door gasket.	1. A torn, flattened, or hardened gasket should be replaced. Position the gasket tightly around the door.
	2. Broken door hinge.	2. Replace the hinge.
	3. Fitting on the water-inlet line leaks or the line is ruptured.	3. Tighten the compression nut to stop the fitting from leaking. If the line is damaged, replace it.
	4. Defective motor seal.	4. If water leaks from around the motor shaft, replace the seal.
	5. Loose hose clamp.	5. Check and tighten all hose clamps.
Dishwasher does not operate	1. Door is not closed and latched.	1. Door must be closed and latch locked.
	2. Cycle selection button is not fully engaged.	2. Depress the cycle button all the way.
	3. Blown fuse or tripped circuit breaker.	3. Replace the bad fuse or reset the circuit breaker. If the fuse blows or the circuit breaker trips again, there is an electrical defect. Call a serviceman immediately. Do not operate the appliance.
	4. Defective door switch.	4. Test the switch with a continuity tester while depressing the switch button. Replace the switch if it is open.
	5. Defective timer.	5. Turn the timer dial by hand very slowly with the door latched and the wash cycle button engaged. If the timer fails to turn the dishwasher on, it is probably defective and must be replaced.
	6. Defective motor.	6. Call in a service technician.
Dishwasher fails to turn off	1. Defective timer.	1. The fill phase should last about 60 seconds. If timer does not move off "Fill," it is probably defective and should be replaced.
	2. Water-inlet valve stuck open.	2. Have a service technician disassemble and clean the valve or replace it.
	3. Clogged water-inlet valve bleed hole.	3. Disassemble valve and clean out bleed hole.
	4. Defective float switch.	4. In those diswashers equipped with a float, check the switch for burned-out contacts.
Dishwasher operates when door is open	1. Faulty door interlock.	1. Replace the door interlock switch.

PROBLEMS	CAUSES	REPAIRS
Dishes stay wet	1. Water too cool.	1. Check the temperature of your home's hot water. It must be at least 140 degrees F.
	2. Dishes stacked incorrectly.	2. Stack the dishes so that there is adequate space around them. Avoid clutter and dishes resting against each other.
	3. Calcium deposits on heater element.	3. Clean the heater element.
	4. Loose connection at heater element.	4. Tighten or repair the loose connection.
	5. Heater element burned out.	5. Replace the heater element.
	6. Inoperative fan motor (some models).	6. Replace the fan motor.
Dishwasher fails to drain	1. The drain hose is kinked or clogged.	1. Remove the drain hose and straighten it; make sure that the hose is not clogged and reinstall it.
	2. Damaged or defective pump.	2. Remove and disassemble the pump. Clean away any clogged material. Be sure that all particles are removed; otherwise, the pump can be damaged.
	3. Stuck timer.	3. If the timer does not advance by itself, it is probably defective. Replace it.
	4. Defective pump motor.	4. Advance the timer to its drain phase. If the motor hums, look for impeller obstructions. If the impeller is free, the pump motor wiring is probably defective. Replace the pump motor.

TRASH COMPACTORS

The trash compactor, the newest of the major appliances, has a drawer or container made of strong steel into which you place a bag and the trash. Some compactors must be equipped with special plastic-lined bags, while others can use ordinary grocery bags. When you turn the compactor to the start position, the motor turns a sprocket gear which in turn drives two threaded shafts. At the top of these shafts is a ram that is attached to two nuts. The rotation of the shaft within these nuts causes the ram to move downward into the closed compartment.

The ram can exert a force of 2000 to 4000 pounds as it moves down on the trash within the container. A switching circuit, designed to make the motor go in the opposite direction, takes the ram back up to the top of its travel when its compacting job is accomplished. At the top, the ram comes in contact with a switch arm that turns the compactor off, ending the cycle until you press the start button again.

Safety is a prime concern to manufacturers of trash compactors. The storage drawer in many models is designed to be especially difficult for a child to open; it must be lifted somewhat before it can be pulled forward. In addition, a key-lock switch prevents the compactor from being operated unless someone inserts the key in the switch. Finally, the compactor will not work unless the drawer is closed completely. Sometimes an object forces the drawer to twist and begin to open as the ram depresses the garbage. If this happens, the compactor will shut off. To restart the appliance, you must push the drawer

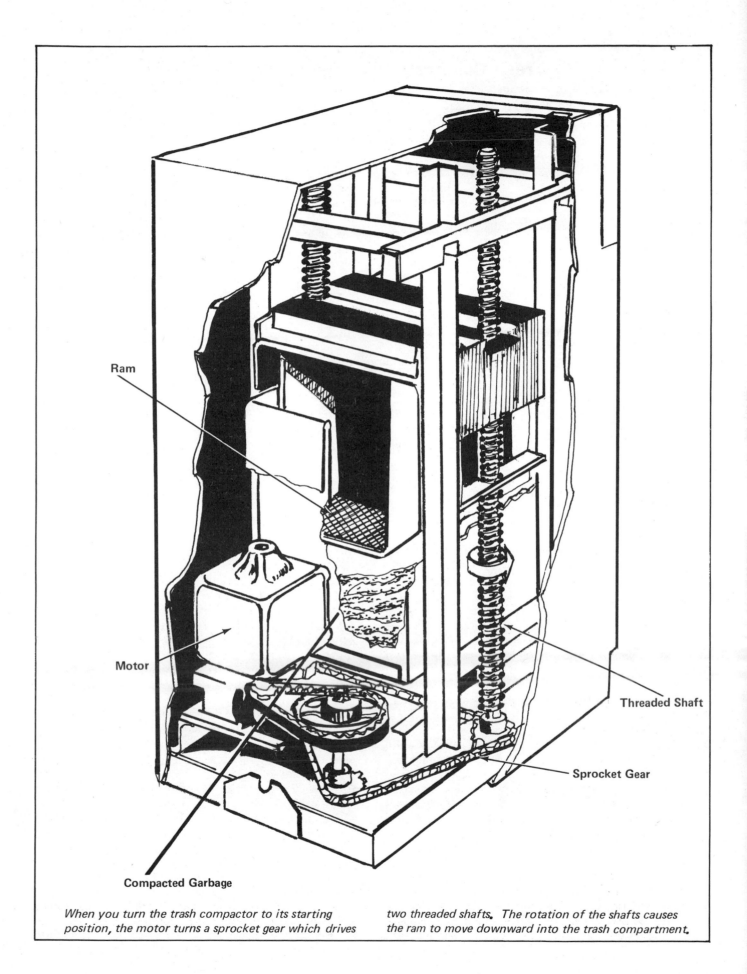

Ram

Motor

Compacted Garbage

Threaded Shaft

Sprocket Gear

When you turn the trash compactor to its starting position, the motor turns a sprocket gear which drives two threaded shafts. The rotation of the shafts causes the ram to move downward into the trash compartment.

Trash Compactor Troubleshooting Chart

Caution: *Unplug appliance before inspecting or repairing. Do not reconnect power until job is completed or while any wiring connections are exposed.*

PROBLEMS	CAUSES	REPAIRS
Trash compactor fails to start	1. Power disconnected.	1. Make sure that power cord is plugged into the wall socket.
	2. Blown fuse or tripped circuit breaker.	2. Replace the fuse or reset the circuit breaker. If trouble recurs, call an electrician.
	3. Front door safety switch has failed.	3. Test the switch for continuity; replace the switch if it is open.
	4. Rear drawer safety switch, safety lock switch, start switch, or relay has failed.	4. Test each part in turn for continuity; replace any defective parts.
Ram does not reach trash for compression	1. Lack of lubrication on screws.	1. Lubricate with special trash compactor grease.
	2. Ram binding.	2. Clean out posts; look for bent parts.
	3. Drive chain too tight.	3. Adjust the belt for tension.
Ram fails to reverse	1. Defective relay, directional switch or safety switch.	1. Test each component, and replace if necessary.
	2. Defective ram stop pads.	2. Replace the pads.

back into position and press the start switch. The ram will travel upward, at which point you can open the container drawer and rearrange the trash. Then, you can start the entire cycle all over again.

There are few service or maintenance procedures you can perform on a compactor. Remove and clean the ram every month to prevent odors from arising, and clean the container drawer at regular intervals even though little garbage escapes the disposable bags. If you find it necessary to remove the drive mechanism for service, be sure to apply an extreme high-pressure lubricant before putting the mechanism back into operation. If you leave the drive mechanism alone, however, its lubricant should last the lifetime of the appliance.

Exercise the utmost care when emptying the trash compactor's disposable bags. Broken glass can puncture the plastic or paper bag and inflict injury. The best and safest method of handling compacted garbage is to place the bag into a separate container before transporting it to the garbage can. Try not to handle the trash bag directly.

GARBAGE DISPOSERS

Garbage disposers are relatively simple devices designed to eliminate wet garbage down your kitchen sink drain. The upper portion of the disposer bolts to the sink flange or sink outlet in place of the normal outlet, and water and food matter pass into a container located directly below the outlet. At the bottom of the garbage disposer container is a flywheel which is mounted directly to the motor shaft.

When you turn on the disposer, the flywheel spins at around 1725 rpm. The centrifugal force of the spinning disk throws the food against the sides of the container with some force. At the outer edge of the disk is a hardened steel ring — called a shredder — which contains several sets of cutting edges. The food waste hits the shredder ring and is ground into tiny pieces. Some flywheels have pivoting weights on them to hammer away at stubborn foods; others have a flat flywheel which is designed to direct the food to the cutting edges of the shredder.

When the particles are ground small enough to pass through the openings between the shredder ring and the flywheel, a stream of cold water flushes these particles down into the drain line. You should always have the cold water running when you use your disposer; it will flush the garbage particles away as fast as they are ground. You must use only cold water when you operate your disposer. Hot water temporarily liquifies grease which then solidifies further down the drain line. A drain that is coated with grease collects other disposer waste until you have a clog of major proportions to try to eliminate.

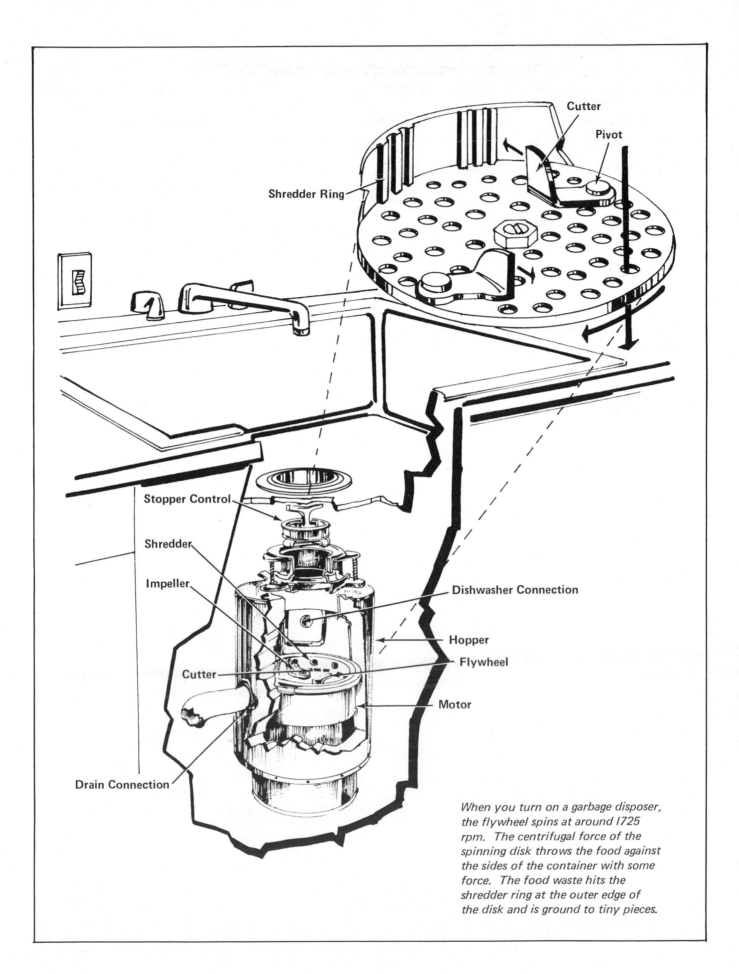

Cutter

Pivot

Shredder Ring

Stopper Control

Shredder

Impeller

Cutter

Drain Connection

Dishwasher Connection

Hopper

Flywheel

Motor

When you turn on a garbage disposer, the flywheel spins at around 1725 rpm. The centrifugal force of the spinning disk throws the food against the sides of the container with some force. The food waste hits the shredder ring at the outer edge of the disk and is ground to tiny pieces.

Garbage Disposers Troubleshooting Chart

Caution: Unplug appliance before inspecting or repairing. Do not reconnect power until job is completed or while any wiring connections are exposed.

PROBLEMS	CAUSES	REPAIRS
Disposer fails to operate	1. No voltage to receptacle or blown fuse on line.	1. Test the receptacle with a table lamp. If the disposer is wired directly, replace the blown circuit fuse.
	2. Overload protector kicked out.	2. Depress the reset button, which is usually located on the bottom of the disposer.
	3. Foreign object jamming the impeller.	3. Free the foreign object by inserting a wooden stick (broom handle) and prying against the jammed impeller.
	4. Defective relay switch, capacitor, or motor.	4. Call in a service technician.
Disposer leaks	1. Loose sink flange connections.	1. Check the connections and tighten.
	2. Impeller or seals leaking.	2. Call in a service technician.
Disposer makes excessive noise	1. Foreign object in disposer.	1. Remove the foreign object.
Disposer emits a foul odor	1. Insufficient flushing of food particles.	1. Grind up a hopper full of ice, followed by lemon. Flush using plenty of cold water.
Water fails to flow out	1. Clogged drain line.	1. Clean the drain line, but do not use a chemical cleaner. Use only a special cleaner made for garbage disposer purposes.
	2. Worn shredder.	2. Call in a service technician.

Cold water, on the other hand, allows the grease to form into tiny globules and wash out of the disposer and through the drain pipe without sticking to anything along the route.

There are two basic types of disposers. The continuous-feed type is connected to a wall switch. You turn on the switch as you push the garbage into the appliance's hopper — a process usually accomplished with some sort of a spatula. Continuous-feed disposers have a guard, usually made of rubber, at the top of the disposer inlet. In contrast, the batch-feed disposer has a special stopper which must be inserted and turned to a locked position before you can operate the disposer. You load the garbage into a batch-feed disposer before you start the grinding. Then, you lock the top in place and turn on the cold water. Batch-feed disposers are generally regarded as safer than continuous-feed models because it is nearly impossible to put your hand in a batch-feed unit while it is running.

There is more qualitative difference be-tween the top-of-the-line and the lower-priced dis-posers than is the case with most other appliances. Smaller motors and fewer features (such as reversing switch) are signs of less-expensive units. In some cases, moreover, the designs and materials cannot match those of the more expensive disposers, and the inexpensive disposers enjoy a much shorter life expectancy. At the upper price level, you are more likely to find disposers with larger hoppers, more powerful motors, and superior sound insulation.

Some disposers have automatic reversing. The disposer flywheel turns first in one direction, and then in the opposite direction the next time that you start the appliance. Reversing helps to keep the blade sharp, and it increases the operational life of the disposer. When disposers equipped with auto-matic reversing become jammed with a foreign object, their flywheels rock back and forth to throw off the jammed object. Other disposers have a manual reversing switch which you can flip to reverse the direction of the flywheel's rotation.

The cardinal rule for disposer operation is to put in only the type of garbage capable of being ground by the particular disposer model you own. The list of disposable garbage items varies from one company to another, depending on the design and construction of their disposers. Be sure to check your instruction manual before you operate any garbage disposer; familiarize yourself thoroughly with the things that your disposer can and cannot accept.

Some of the things that are definitely taboo are metal objects (such as bottle tops, spoons, forks, etc.), glass, paper, plastic, and rubber. Not only are these likely to jam the disposer, but they can also clog the drain line. Most disposers can grind bones; in fact, bones are good for your disposer because they help clean away detergent film as well as the citric acid deposits left after you grind fruit peelings.

No matter how well you care for it, though, sooner or later your disposer will become jammed with a foreign object. Before you take any corrective action whatsoever, be sure to unplug the disposer. Try to remove the object directly if you can. Some disposers have a wrench which you can insert through the bottom of the housing to turn the flywheel. Turn the power off, insert the wrench, and rock it to both sides until you free the jam.

If your disposer did not come with such a wrench, you can insert a wooden stick — a broom handle works well — through the mouth of the disposer. Use the stick to pry against the jam in both directions, and you are almost sure to dislodge the intruder. Remove the foreign object from the hopper before you turn the disposer on again. A pair of ice tongs is handy for such tasks. Never — under any circumstances — put your hand into the mouth of any disposer. Obey this rule no matter what type of machine you own.

Be sure to use plenty of cold water when you run your disposer, and follow the manufacturer's instructions for getting rid of odors. Usually, grinding a hopper full of ice cubes, followed by a whole lemon, is quite effective in deodorizing your disposer.

CLOTHES WASHERS

To understand how an automatic clothes washer operates, you must familiarize yourself with the function of three basic components: the timer, the motor, and the solenoid.

A timer is nothing more than a group of switches that turn electrical components on and off. These switches are moved by a cam which is rotated by the timer's motor drive. Timer motors are called synchronous because they are timed to the unvarying cycles of current in the power supply. It is not possible to use the synchronous motor's movement without modification, however. The motor's movement is relatively slow, too slow to handle the number of contacts that must be sequenced or

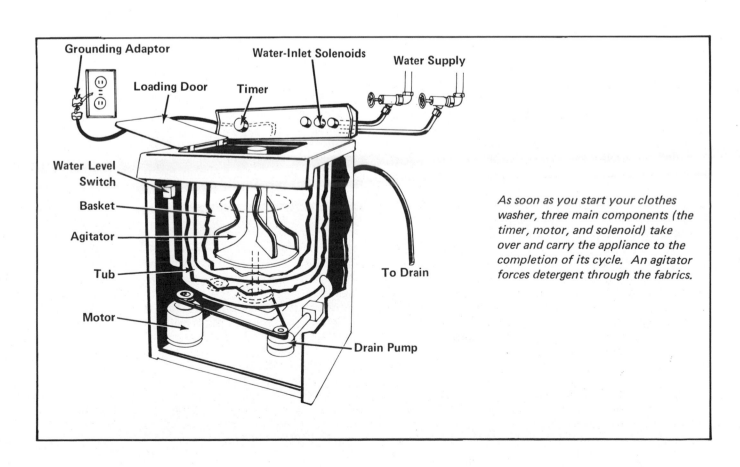

As soon as you start your clothes washer, three main components (the timer, motor, and solenoid) take over and carry the appliance to the completion of its cycle. An agitator forces detergent through the fabrics.

opened and closed together. Therefore, an escapement mechanism is attached to the synchronous motor. Though nothing more than a gear train with a spring mechanism, the escapement mechanism moves the timer cam in jerks rather than in a slow smooth movement. The jerking action causes the contacts to open and close rapidly, increasing their life and providing proper sequencing.

The second primary component is the motor. Usually a split-phase or capacitor type, the motor is generally reversible. The machine's design utilizes a special spring in the transmission to turn the motor in one direction for agitation and in the reverse direction for the spin cycle.

The third essential component is the solenoid. A solenoid is a coil of wire, formed to concentrate the magnetic force that surrounds individual wires when current flows through them. Depending upon the type and size of the windings and the amount of current involved, the magnetic force exerted can be quite strong. The solenoid uses this force to move an armature or plunger. In this way, the solenoid transforms electrical energy to mechanical motion. Solenoids can control many phases of appliance operation, and they are used for several different purposes in automatic washers.

As soon as you start your washer, these three components — timer, motor, and solenoid — take over and carry the appliance through its complete cycle. Turning the timer to the starting position energizes a solenoid in the water-inlet valve. This valve is located at the point where the hose enters the washer; in fact, the hose is attached to the threaded portion of the valve. There is one solenoid for the hot water and one for cold water. When the timer turns the hot water solenoid on, a plunger inside the valve pulls away from an opening to allow the hot water to flow through. When the timer deenergizes the solenoid, a spring returns the plunger to its original position, and water pressure from the line provides the force to close the valve. In the cold water line, the same process takes place when the coil is energized. When you set the washer for warm water, both hot and cold solenoids are energized, and both water-inlet valves open. The passageways inside the valves are sized to provide the proper proportion of hot and cold water required for warm water washing.

As the washer tub fills to the proper level, the timer actuates another switch to halt the water flow. In most cases, this switch is mounted to the rear of a diaphragm. On the opposite side of the sealed diaphragm unit, a tube runs to a pocket near the bottom of the tub. As water rises within the tub, the weight of the water exerts increasing pressure upon the air trapped within the tube. When the water reaches the proper level, this pressure is sufficient to allow the diaphragm to move the switch contacts. As a result, the contacts controlling the water-inlet valve open, the contacts controlling the motor circuit close, and the machine begins its wash cycle.

The vast majority of modern automatic washers use an agitator to force the detergent and water solution through the fibers of the clothing fabrics. Washer baskets and agitators are designed to provide good water movement; it is the water movement — not the friction between the agitator and clothing — that accomplishes the cleaning. That is a good point to remember when you are loading clothes into the washer. Regardless of the type of agitator, water should circulate freely in the tub, and the clothing should be able to move well in the water. If you can see active motion, then you know that your clothing load is suitable. On the other hand, if your clothing gets tangled in a pile with little evidence of good movement between water and clothing, then you know that you have an overloaded condition in your washer. Remove the excess clothing to obtain good cleaning results.

Following the wash cycle, the machine must remove the soil- and grease-laden wash water. Some machines, primarily those that have a perforated basket (holes in both sides and bottom), pump the water out before the basket starts to spin. Washing machines that have a solid basket start spinning while the water is still in the tub. Centrifugal force pushes the water up and over the top edge of the basket.

There is a difference, by the way, between a basket and a tub. The basket is the inner part in which you place the clothing. The tub is the outer part which you seldom see. It may be the inside of the cabinet, or it may be a separate container; in either case, however, it is the tub that holds the water until the machine pumps it out through the drain line.

After the washer pumps the water out — or after the wash cycle, depending upon the type of mechanism — the machine enters its spin cycle. The basket begins to revolve faster and faster until the clothing is forced against the basket's sides. Most washers spin between 500 and 600 rpm (some go as high as 1200 rpm), and the centrifugal force that is generated causes much of the water to leave the fabric.

A second fill period with clear, clean water follows the initial spin cycle. The second fill period is called the rinse cycle, and during it the clothes are agitated briefly before the water is again pumped away to flush any remaining soap and soil. During the initial spin cycle and briefly again after the rinse cycle, water is sprayed into the machine to help remove the detergent and grime. After these rinsing cycles are completed, the washing machine tub spins for several minutes just prior to shutting off. The powerful spinning action is designed to eliminate as much moisture from the clothing as possible; your clothes are then ready to hang on a line or to be placed in the dryer.

Several interesting mechanisms, depending upon the washer make and model, are used to provide the agitating and spinning actions. While all

For apartments or homes where appliance space is at a minimum, a portable clothes washer can be ideal.

brands differ in many respects, these mechanisms can usually be grouped in either one of two basic categories. The first type of washer mechanism involves a reversible motor and torque springs. When a torque spring — simply a tight steel spring placed around a shaft — is turned in one direction, the spring merely slips; it fails to grip the shaft. Turn the torque spring in the other direction, however, and it grips the shaft tightly. Two of these springs used in conjunction with each other can drive separate parts of the washer's operating mechanisms. One spring grips the shaft that drives the agitator, while the other allows the spin mechanism to be free. Then, the situation is reversed: the first spring frees the agitator mechanism, and the second torque spring spins the basket.

Inside the gear box there is a mechanism designed to convert the rotary motion of the motor to the oscillating or pulsating motion of the agitator. The conversion process usually involves either an off-center pin on a drive gear or an eccentric drive.

The spin mechanism itself is usually a simple tube which surrounds the agitator shaft. The basket, which is attached to this outer tube, must revolve when the tube begins to turn. The spin tube is independent of the inner agitator shaft, and it is generally separated from it by sleeve bearings. Solenoids shift the gear box in and out of action to provide agitation and to engage the clutch that provides the spinning operation. In most cases, the agitator shaft and the spin tube arrangements are similar to those used on machines that employ motor reversal.

In addition to overloading your automatic washer with clothing, it is also possible to overload the machine with detergent. The amount of detergent that you should use depends on the type of machine you own and the water conditions in your area. Try to keep the suds level to no more than one inch during the wash cycle, and watch the spin cycle for evidence of oversudsing. An excess of detergent can cause a suds buildup between the basket and the tub, which then acts like a brake on the surface of the basket. Washing results suffer if the machine is prevented from rinsing the clothing thoroughly. In fact, too little detergent will clean your clothes better than too much detergent.

Most automatic washers have strainers to prevent foreign matter from entering the water-inlet valves, and these screens can become clogged. If water enters your machine slowly or not at all, check the valve screen first. There are usually two screens on each inlet line. One is built into the hose washer at the faucet end, and the other is positioned just inside the threaded portion of the inlet valve at the point where the hose is attached. The screens are made of stainless steel, and you can take them out and brush away any foreign matter with an old toothbrush.

Many of the newer automatic clothes washers have dispensers to put detergent, bleach, and

A solenoid concentrates the magnetic force of individual wires to move an armature or plunger. Solenoids are used for many different purposes on clothes washers.

fabric conditioner into the water at the correct time. The dispensers are more than just added frills; they enhance the effectiveness of the cleansing and conditioning chemicals. For instance, bleach and detergent should never be put into the machine together; bleach tends to inhibit the detergent's cleaning action. A dispenser can add the bleach slowly near the end of the wash cycle. Fabric conditioner, of course, should be added during the deep rinse cycle, and a dispenser makes it easy to add the conditioner at exactly the right time. Be sure to maintain your dispensers properly. Put a cup of hot water into each one about once a month to keep them clean, and if you ever inadvertently mix additives in a dispenser, flush the dispenser immediately.

When inspecting an automatic washer, be sure to unplug the cord before lifting the top or removing a service panel. Check the belts; they should be adjusted so that they can be depressed only about one half inch between the pulleys. You can usually adjust the belts by loosening the bolts that attach the motor unit to the base or subframe of the washer.

The drain hose should be tailored to the washer's standpipe. If the hose becomes partially crimped, it can block the waste water's flow. A new drain hose can often support itself, but after hot water has passed through it, the hose can sag or crimp and reduce — or even stop — water flow. If you cut the hose to fit the washer standpipe, you eliminate the possibility of a sag or crimp impeding the passage of waste water to the drain.

All washers should have an external ground wire leading from a clamp on the cold water line to a screw on the cabinet of the machine. The ground wire provides vital protection against electrical shock. Another important point to consider is that the standpipe into which the washer drain hose empties must be sufficiently high to prevent siphoning from

Clothes Washers Troubleshooting Chart

Caution: *Unplug appliance before inspecting or repairing. Do not reconnect power until job is completed or while any wiring connections are exposed.*

PROBLEMS	CAUSES	REPAIRS
Washer does not fill with water	1. Water shut-off valves on supply pipes closed.	1. Open the valves.
	2. Water-inlet hoses kinked or knotted.	2. Straighten out the hoses.
	3. Clogged water-intake screens.	3. Remove the screens and clean out the sediment.
	4. Defective water-valve solenoid.	4. Remove the leads from the valve, and test them with a continuity tester. If the solenoid coil is open, replace it.
	5. Defective water valve.	5. Disassemble the water valve and inspect all parts for damage. Replace a bad part with a new one, if possible. If not, replace the entire valve.
	6. Defective timer.	6. Test the timer with a continuity tester, and replace the timer if it is faulty. Be sure to replace the lead wires correctly.
	7. Defective water temperature switch or water level pressure switch.	7. Test the switches with a continuity tester and replace if faulty.
	8. Open circuit in timer, in water solenoid valve coil, or in connecting wires.	8. Once you are sure that the machine is unplugged, use a continuity tester to check for a complete circuit from the line cord plug prong to the solenoid; also make a continuity check between the two solenoid terminals. There should be continuity from "source to load" — from the line cord plug to the motor lead wire — when the timer is set to wash. Be sure that washer is unplugged.
Agitator does not work	1. Broken drive belt.	1. Replace with a new belt.
	2. Drive belt is too loose and slipping.	2. Tighten the belt until the belt tension is such that the belt can be deflected no more than 1/2 of an inch.
	3. Defective transmission.	3. Place the control knob timer in its "Wash" position. Remove the drive belt, and turn the transmission pulley by hand in the direction of agitation, which is generally clockwise. If the agitator is not driven by this action, the transmission is probably bad and should be overhauled or replaced.

PROBLEMS	CAUSES	REPAIRS
	4. Defective timer or water level pressure switch.	4. Test the timer and switch with a continuity tester while tub is full of water. Replace faulty parts.
Water drains from machine during wash and rinse cycles instead of at the end of the cycle	1. Drain hose may be positioned lower than the water level in basket. This creates a vacuum and water siphons out.	1. Reposition the drain hose so that it is higher than the highest water level in the basket.
Machine does not spin at all or does not spin at correct speed	1. Broken drive belt.	1. Replace with a new belt.
	2. Slipping drive belt.	2. Tighten the belt.
	3. Loose motor drive pulley.	3. Tighten the pulley set screw.
	4. Defective drive clutch.	4. With washer unplugged, dial the control knob (timer) to its "Spin" position. Remove the drive belt and turn the clutch by hand. If there is a strong resistance, the clutch is bad and should be replaced.
	5. Spin brake does not release or transmission is frozen.	5. The spin brake and transmission are attached. Place the control knob (timer) in its "Spin" position. Remove the drive belt, and turn the brake stator. It should move freely. If the brake stator binds, the brake assembly or transmission is defective. Have one or both repaired.
	6. Defective timer.	6. Test according to manufacturer's recommended procedure and replace if faulty.
	7. Open circuit.	7. Use a continuity tester to check for complete circuit from line cord to solenoid terminals.
	8. Too much detergent.	8. Reduce the amount of detergent you use.
	9. Clutch needs adjusting (disc type).	9. Adjust the nut or the clutch actuating shaft.
Motor does not operate	1. Power cord disconnected.	1. Make sure that power cord is plugged into a wall outlet.
	2. Blown fuse or tripped circuit breaker.	2. Replace the fuse or reset the circuit breaker. If the fuse blows or the circuit breaker trips again, disconnect the appliance. Do not operate it until an electrician or appliance serviceman checks it. A malfunction exists that could cause a fire.

PROBLEMS	CAUSES	REPAIRS
	3. Defective lid switch.	3. Most newer washing machines have a safety switch which is activated by the lid; the machine turns off automatically when the lid is raised during operation. Test this switch with the continuity tester. Replace the switch if it is open when lid button is depressed.
	4. Defective timer.	4. Test the timer according to the manufacturer's recommended procedure, and replace it if it is faulty.
	5. Defective motor.	5. Most washing machines are protected by an internal overload circuit breaker which turns the appliance off if the motor overheats. If the motor cannot be started 30 minutes after this protective device turns the machine off, one of the following conditions exist: (a) If the motor has switched off as the washing machine went into its "Spin" position, the reason for the problem may not be the motor, but rather the clutch, transmission, or brake. To determine which part is faulty, remove the drive belts, set the control knob at its "Spin" position, and turn on the machine. If the motor operates, there is no motor problem. Isolate the failure to the clutch, transmission, or brake. (b) If the motor operates in its "Spin" position but not in its "Wash" position (or vice versa), the cause of the problem may be a bad timer or a defective lid switch. Check these two components before you decide that the motor is defective.
Water does not drain out of washer	1. Kinked or knotted drain hose.	1. Straighten out the drain hose.
	2. Broken drive belt.	2. Replace with a new drive belt.
	3. Slipping drive belt.	3. Tighten the belt.
	4. Locked pump.	4. Remove the pump and inspect. Replace it if necessary.

the machine. Most manufacturers recommend a minimum height of 34 inches, and most plumbing codes dictate the same. If your standpipe is less than 34 inches, you can extend it with a plastic pipe of slightly larger diameter; merely clamp the plastic extension pipe tightly to the existing standpipe.

If your washer should develop a leak, you can often trace the source after the water has dried by looking for detergent stains on the underside of the machine. Leak repairs usually involve replacing or tightening a hose clamp or replacing a part.

CLOTHES DRYERS

The clothes dryer consists of a cabinet surrounding a motor-driven drum. Clothing placed inside the drum tumbles through air which has been warmed by a heater and pulled into and through the drum by an exhaust fan. These three basic components — heat, air flow, and tumbling action — must be present for a clothes dryer to operate properly. Actually, the clothes dryer is a very simple appliance. When it is operating properly, it can dry your clothing quickly and safely, but the appliance must be kept in proper operating condition and it must be used correctly.

The motor that drives the drum is usually located at the base of the dryer. You can get at it by removing either the front panel or the rear service panel, but be sure to unplug the dryer before attempting any motor service or repairs. In the case of a gas dryer, be sure that the gas line is turned off before you open up the appliance or pull it away from the wall.

The motor drives a belt, which in most newer dryers completely surrounds the outside of the drum. Many of these belts have an odd appearance — almost flat like a rubber band. If you look at the belt closely, however, you can see that it has a number of grooves on one side to give the belt great gripping power. Near the point where the belt is attached to the small motor pulley, a spring-loaded wheel (called an idler) maintains tension on the belt as the drum turns. Since the drum itself acts as a very large pulley and the motor has a very small one, tremendous speed reduction is obtained. Most drums rotate at around 50 rpm, any faster and centrifugal force would tend to hold the clothing against the side of the drum rather than allowing it to tumble.

The dryer's heat source can be either an electric heating element or a gas burner. In either case, the heat source is usually located within a box that has both an inlet and an outlet. Air flows in through the box where it is heated, and then it is

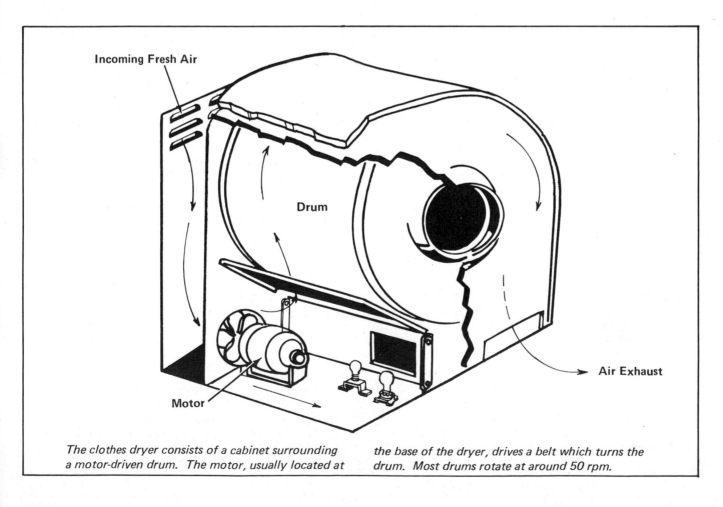

The clothes dryer consists of a cabinet surrounding a motor-driven drum. The motor, usually located at the base of the dryer, drives a belt which turns the drum. Most drums rotate at around 50 rpm.

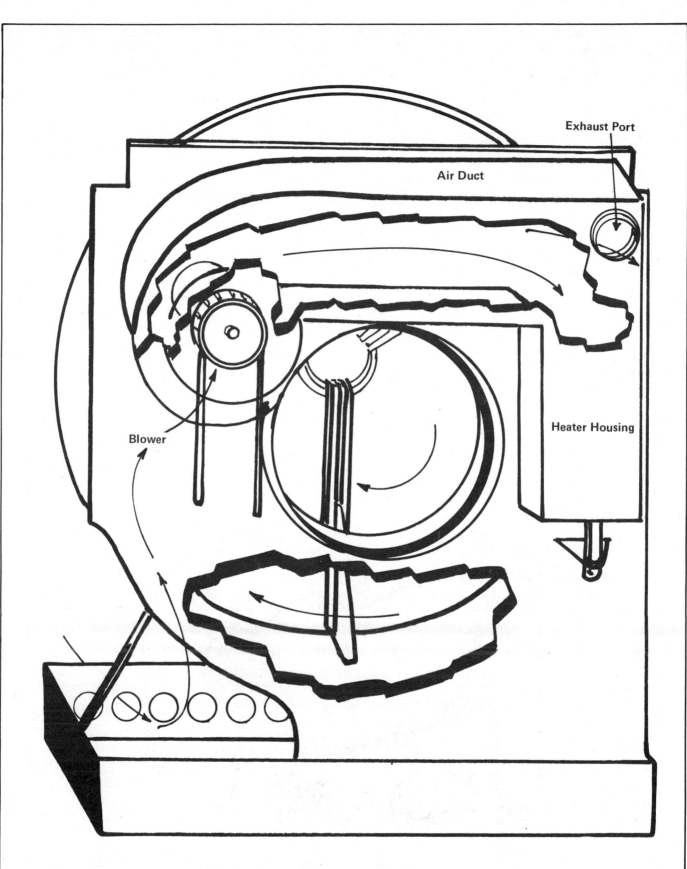

Exhaust Port

Air Duct

Heater Housing

Blower

Air flows in and is heated by a burner or a heating element, and then it is blown into the drum by a fan. The heated air flows into the drum, where it absorbs moisture from the clothing, and it is then exhausted to the outside of your home through the vent. Most dryers are set to operate at around 145 degrees F.

blown into the drum by a fan. Since the drum is a sealed container when the dryer door is closed, the exhaust fan must pull air through the opening and into the heater box to replace that expelled by the fan. The heated air flows into the drum, where it absorbs moisture from the clothing, and it is then exhausted to the outside of your home through the vent.

The heat level is quite important. Heat must be controlled at the proper temperature for the type of clothing that is in the dryer. Most dryers have one thermostatic control set to operate around 145 degrees F., but some dryers offer an adjustable thermostat which you can set according to the nature of the load you are drying. The adjustable thermostat can range from 120 degrees for delicate clothing to 155 degrees for heavy cottons and linens. You can check your dryer's temperature by inserting a candy or meat thermometer in the exhaust vent at the point where the vent is attached to the dryer. The machine's temperature sensors are usually located within the exhaust duct, just inside the dryer.

There is another thermostat in your dryer, but it is there for safety purposes only. The safety thermostat shuts off the heating element or burner when the temperature in the dryer exceeds 200 degrees. Normally, your dryer will never even approach 200 degrees; it gets that hot only in cases where the thermostat sticks, the heating element becomes grounded, or the air flow through the dryer is blocked.

Most dryers that were built within the past few years have sealed-for-life lubrication. If you ever disassemble the dryer for any reason, however, you must be sure that all bearing surfaces are lubricated; use the manufacturer's recommended lubricant. One important spot to check is around the front edge. The drum of many modern dryers is supported on rollers at the rear, while in front the flange of the door opening serves as a bearing surface. If the surface appears to be dry, lubricate it according to the manufacturer's instructions.

One of the most important preventative maintenance tasks you can do for your dryer is to clean the lint filter prior to drying every load. If the filter becomes completely clogged, some lint can escape and create jamming problems elsewhere in the dryer. Even a partial blockage reduces the dryer's efficiency and limits its capabilities. Most importantly, though, a clogged dryer can be a fire hazard. Lint from many fabrics — particularly synthetics — is highly combustible.

The vent is designed to carry heat and moisture away from the dryer to the outside of the house. While the vent may seem to waste a great deal of heat which could be put to use, remember that the warm air is heavy with moisture after it passes through the dryer. Were this air to be recirculated through the dryer, the appliance's efficiency would suffer greatly, since the air simply could not hold much additional moisture. Moreover, the same air is circulated through the dryer motor to help cool it. The hotter the air is, the hotter the motor will run.

Check to see what types of venting materials are allowed in your community. Many hardware and building-supply stores carry kits with which you can do a good job of venting the dryer yourself. Keep the runs as short and with as few bends as possible, and always place a vent cap on the outside to prevent small animals from entering the duct.

Although it is very tempting to place large quantities of clothing in the big drum, remember that the clothing needs a great deal of space for tumbling. Never dry more than a single washer load in a single dryer load, and never try to bake your clothes completely dry. Most clothes should be allowed to retain a slight amount of moisture.

Once a year unplug the dryer or turn off the gas supply, remove the service panel, and vacuum away any lint or dust in the vicinity of the motor. Regular cleaning keeps lint away from the bearings, and it helps maintain clean air passageways. It also reduces the possibility of a fire.

Clothes Dryers Troubleshooting Chart

Caution: Unplug appliance before inspecting or repairing. Do not reconnect power until job is completed or while any wiring connections are exposed. If you suspect a leak in a gas appliance, turn off the gas supply, extinguish all open flames, open windows or doors, and leave the area. Never search for a leak with a match or any other sort of open flame. Call an authorized technician or your utility company for a complete check before operating the appliance.

PROBLEMS	CAUSES	REPAIRS
Dryer fails to run	1. Blown fuse.	1. Replace fuses in the dryer circuit.
	2. Broken belt.	2. Unplug the dryer, remove the service panel, and replace the broken belt with the manufacturer's specified part. Be sure to apply proper tension to the new belt.

PROBLEMS	CAUSES	REPAIRS
	3. Defective door safety switch.	3. Check the switch with a continuity tester. Replace the switch or adjust the linkage.
	4. Defective timer.	4. Check the contacts to the heating element, and replace the timer if the contacts are open when they should be closed.
Dryer runs, but there is no heat	1. Insufficient voltage reaching appliance.	1. Replace both fuses to the appliance.
	2. Thermostat(s) open.	2. Test with a continuity tester when the machine is cool and replace any defective thermostat.
	3. Thermostat or timer turned to air position.	3. Set the thermostat or timer to the correct position.
Clothes not drying sufficiently	1. Lint filter clogged.	1. Remove and clean the lint filter.
	2. Dryer is overloaded with clothing.	2. Dry only one washer load at each dryer cycle.
	3. Timer set incorrectly.	3. Set timer for longer drying time.
	4. Clothing too wet when placed in dryer from washer.	4. Check the washer's operation.
	5. Circuitry to heating element open.	5. Test the circuitry with a continuity tester, and replace any defective component.
Dryer runs noisily	1. Lint buildup behind drum.	1. Unplug the dryer and remove the lint buildup. This can sometimes be accomplished by pressing a stiff brush through the perforations in the drum.
	2. Bearings either worn or in need of lubrication.	2. Check bearings; clean and lubricate them if necessary.
	3. Slipping belts.	3. Check belt tension and adjust it properly. Wraparound belts must be properly tensioned by the idler.
	4. Lint in blower fan.	4. Remove the fan and clean the lint from it.

ELECTRIC RANGES

Most electric ranges employ a sheath-type enclosed nichrome heating element to provide a controlled amount of heat to the cooking surface and to the oven cavity. The heating elements on the top of the range are shaped to make the maximum amount of contact with the bottom of your pots and pans. It is quite important that your cooking utensils be flat and in good condition, however. Otherwise, the pan can produce "hot spots" in the element, and hot spots reduce the life of the element as well as yield poor cooking results. The cook-top elements — or surface units as they are called — can usually be removed easily. On many newer ranges, in fact, the surface units simply plug into a special receptacle at the rear; while on some other ranges, the units are hinged to make their wiring accessible.

There are two types of surface units. One type of surface unit contains two elements, an outer coil and an inner coil, the outer coil is usually of a higher wattage than the inner coil. The unit has a

The oven has a capillary-tube thermostat to detect and maintain the proper temperature levels. The surface units (below) can usually be removed easily. In fact, on many newer ranges, the surface units simply plug into a special receptacle.

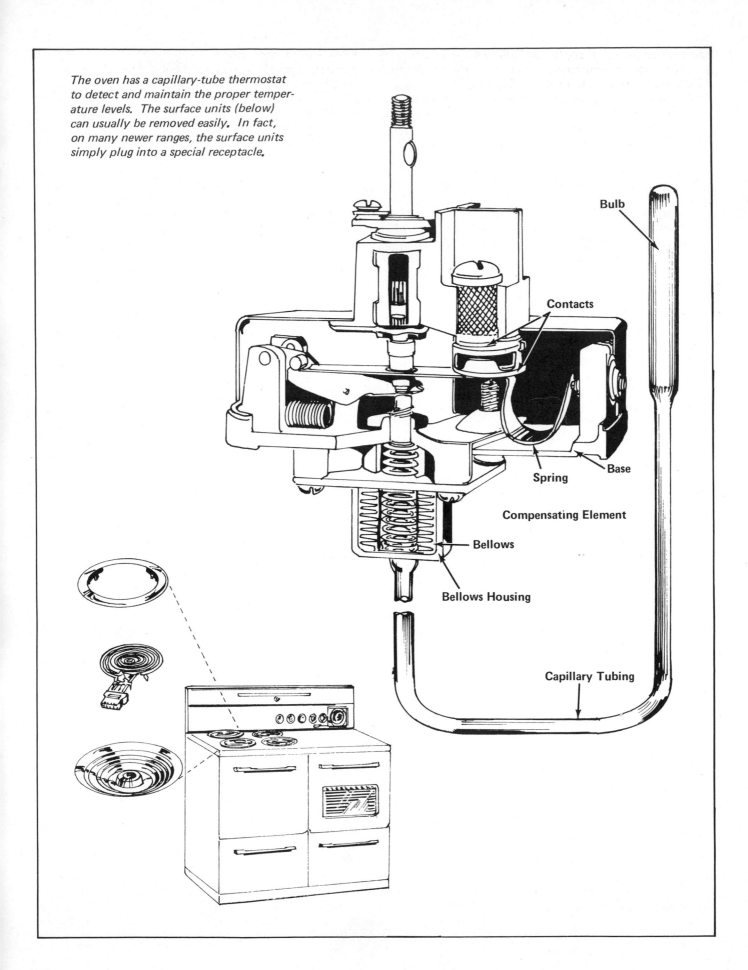

Bulb

Contacts

Base

Spring

Compensating Element

Bellows

Bellows Housing

Capillary Tubing

switch designed to apply the full 240-volt power supply to one or both coils, or to reduce the power to 120 volts to one or both coils. This type of surface unit, therefore, allows you to select from a wide range of heat settings.

Most of the newer ranges feature the other type of surface unit which includes an "infinite heat" control. Such a control possesses an internal bimetal strip that acts like a timer. A small heater within the switch causes the bimetal to move when you turn the burner on. At low heat levels, the bimetal opens a set of contacts within a relatively short time. At the high end of the heat range, the switch stays open for a shorter time and closed longer, because in the high position the voltage must be on for a greater duration. An infinite heat control allows faster heating, and it also permits a vast range of heat selections.

Some electric ranges include a thermostat control on one of the surface units. Usually a solid state type of resistor, this thermostat changes resistance according to the amount of heat you set on the control. The thermostat control has a heat sensor that rests lightly against the pan bottom, and the control adjusts the element to maintain an exact temperature level at the bottom of the pan. It is absolutely essential, however, that your pan have a flat surface that meets the sensor squarely.

Some new ranges have flat ceramic tops over the elements; heat is transferred from the element through the ceramic material to your pots and pans. Sometimes, separate thermostatically controlled switches are used to provide controlled heat to each section of the flat-top range. Be sure to follow the manufacturer's recommendations for cleaning these ranges, and always treat the ceramic surfaces with great care.

Many surface-element problems are related to a burned-out element or to a poor wiring connection either at the element receptacle or where the wire is attached to the element. You can repair any of these connections easily, but be sure to turn off the power supply and unplug the range before attempting to fix any part of your range.

It is possible for an element's inner coil to be ground to its sheathing. If this happens, the coil can actually burn a hole through the outer surface of the element. Sometimes the hole is visible, but if it is not, test the element with a continuity tester. Should you discover a fault, obtain a replacement element from an appliance parts distributor. Then, record the color of each wire and the terminal to which it is connected before you disassemble the faulty element. Rewiring the replacement element should not offer any problems.

If a wire should break or burn away from the element or receptacle, install a special high-temperature terminal when you reconnect it. Be sure that all the wiring connections are tight, and if any connections appear to be corroded, polish them with a file or sandpaper until they are bright and shiny. Heat

from a poor connection is usually the cause of such corrosion, and if you fail to clean it, the connection is sure to malfunction once again.

The oven has a capillary-tube thermostat to detect and maintain the proper temperature levels. As pressure builds up within this tube, it acts upon a bellows that is located in the switch to which the thermostat knob is attached. The bellows movement opens and closes a switch to provide the correct temperature at the sensing tube within the oven cavity. When you turn the thermostat knob, you increase or decrease the spring pressure which opposes the bellows force, requiring more or less force to close the contacts. A linkage is provided to make the contacts move quickly and to prevent arcing and burning at their surface.

The thermostat is usually not serviceable; if part of the thermostat fails, the entire control must be replaced. If the thermostat is out of calibration by more than 25 degrees, however, you usually can adjust it. Place a good thermometer as near to the center of the oven as possible, and set the thermostat to a temperature in the medium range. Allow the oven to stabilize for approximately 30 minutes before taking a reading. If there is a great disparity between the thermometer reading and the thermostat setting, remove the thermostat knob and look for a calibration screw; you may find the screw within a hollow shaft or on the front of the control. Turn the screw to correct the thermostat setting. In other electric ranges, the skirt on the back of the thermostat knob is adjustable; loosening a screw and adjusting the position of the skirt allows you to set the thermostat knob indicator to the correct temperature. If the thermostat moves out of calibration again after you adjust it, install a new thermostat.

If a heating element in an oven fails to operate, and you have verified with the continuity tester or by visual inspection that it is defective, remove it from the oven by loosening the mounting screws at the rear of the oven. When you pull the defective element forward, enough connecting wiring should come with it to allow you to remove the wire from the old element and to attach it to the new element. Naturally, the power must be turned off before you attempt such a repair. In addition, make sure that the wiring connections are bright and shiny before you install the new element.

Many ranges have a timer connected to the oven circuit to turn the oven on and off at preset intervals. Although a convenience feature, the timer, ironically, is frequently the cause of people thinking that their ranges are defective. The timer controls can keep the oven from operating if they are inadvertently moved out of position. Therefore, if your oven fails to function, make certain that the timer is in the manual or normal position. It is easy to move the timer controls out of position accidentally when you clean the range.

The outlet and light are usually connected to the 110-volt circuit independent of the other range circuits. Generally, a separate fuse (located beneath the elements) or a circuit breaker (on the control panel) protects the outlet and light circuit. If the outlet or light ever fails to operate, check the condition of the fuse or the position of the circuit breaker.

If the entire range fails to operate — or if it operates only at a low temperature — chances are that one or both of the main fuses in your home's electrical circuit to the range have blown. If they are cartridge-type fuses, you must check them with a continuity tester or replace them with new ones. If the range circuit is protected by a circuit breaker, simply reset it to restore the range's power supply. Of course, you should try to determine why the fuse blew or the circuit breaker tripped.

Self-cleaning ranges burn away any food soils on the oven surfaces by raising the temperature in the oven cavity to 800 or 900 degrees. Besides having special cabinets made with high-density insulation, these ranges also are equipped with special chrome plating on the racks and a special porcelain coating on the inside of the oven cavity. During the high-heat cleaning, the oven's elements are usually connected into a 115-volt circuit to allow them to heat much more slowly than they normally would; slow heating permits proper decomposition of the food soils. A high-limit switch — which may be part of the oven thermostat — controls the heat at the proper level during the self-cleaning process.

If your self-cleaning oven fails to clean properly, check to be sure that you are setting the controls for the proper length of time (usually three hours are required to burn away normal oven grime). You should, of course, wipe away heavy spills before you initiate the cleaning cycle. If you still have a problem, call in a service technician who has the special testing equipment required to examine your oven's high-temperature operation.

Other ranges possess a special coating on the oven liner to help decompose food soils at regular cooking temperatures. These continuous-cleaning ovens use a catalyst in the liner material that reacts with the soil. You must, however, exercise special care with continuous-cleaning ovens. Never use commercial cleaners on the finish, nor attempt to scrub it with an abrasive cleaner. Wipe away heavy soils immediately, before they have a chance to smother the action of the catalytic coating, and avoid damaging the finish in any way; such damage would leave an unprotected area in the oven liner.

Electric Range Troubleshooting Chart

Caution: Unplug appliance before inspecting or repairing. Do not reconnect power until job is completed or while any wiring connections are exposed.

PROBLEMS	CAUSES	REPAIRS
Oven light fails to operate	1. 15-amp fuse blown. 2. Inoperative switch.	1. Replace the fuse. 2. Check for continuity at the switch terminals. If there is no continuity, replace the switch.
Convenience outlet inoperative	1. 15-amp fuse blown. 2. Clock-timer switch. 3. Defective clock-timer switch.	1. Replace the fuse. 2. Set the clock for automatic operation. 3. Check the switch for continuity. If it lacks continuity, replace the clock-timer or the switch (if available).
Single surface element inoperative	1. Burned-out element. 2. Defective terminal block. 3. Loose wires. 4. Defective infinite switch.	1. Check the element for continuity; if it is open, replace it. 2. Replace the terminal block. 3. Clean the terminals and connect the wires. 4. Replace the switch.
Surface element overheats	1. Defective infinite switch.	1. Replace the switch.
Oven will not operate manually	1. Timer not set for manual operation.	1. Set the timer for manual operation.

PROBLEMS	CAUSES	REPAIRS
Self-cleaning oven door will not open	1. Self-cleaning switch is not turned off.	1. If you cannot turn the switch off, it is defective; replace it.
	2. Main circuit breaker tripped or fuse blown.	2. Reset the circuit breaker or replace the fuse.
	3. Door latch motor defective.	3. Check the continuity of the motor and replace it if the motor lacks continuity.
	4. One or more of the following switches is defective: motor limit switch, door switch, self-cleaning switch, oven thermostat.	4. Check the continuity of the switches, and replace any of them that are defective.
	5. Broken or loose wires or terminals.	5. Check for broken or loose wires and repair any that you find.
	6. Cooling period following self-cleaning is not completed.	6. Wait until lock light goes out.
Oven overheats	1. Defective thermostat.	1. Adjust or replace the thermostat.
	2. Relay sticking.	2. Replace the relay.
	3. Defective or miswired limit switch on a self-cleaning oven.	3. Replace the switch or correct the wiring.
	4. Thermostat bulb not installed properly in oven.	4. Install the thermostat bulb correctly.

GAS RANGES

In a gas range, the heat for both the surface burners and the oven emanates from an open flame. The fuel may be either natural gas or one of several types of bottled gas, but the operation in either case is the same. The gas burner operates by combining the fuel from the supply line with the correct proportion of air for burning that is thorough and clean. The fuel enters the burner assembly through an orifice, which is simply an opening sized to provide the proper amount of gas flow. The gas stream pulls air in through an open shutter behind the orifice, and as the mixture flows on through the burner tube to the burner itself, the air and gas mix thoroughly. By the time it reaches the burner, the air/gas mixture is ready to meet the pilot or the burner flame. Burning then occurs with an odorless and soot-free flame.

Air must be mixed with the fuel supply in the proper proportion to provide a clean-burning and efficient flame. You can judge the quality of the air/fuel mixture by observing the flame. If the flame is yellow, you know that there is insufficient air; if the flame tends to pull away from the burner, you know that there is too much air. You can regulate the quantity of air by adjusting the shutter, which is located at the point where the burner meets a pipe near the front of the range. Merely loosen a screw, adjust the shutter to render the correct flame, and then retighten the screw.

How do you adjust an air shutter? Close the shutter until the flame turns yellow, and then open the shutter slowly until the yellow tips of the flame just disappear. You should see a distinct cone-shaped flame with soft blue tips. The flame is hottest at the points of the tips, and coolest at their base.

The heat output from each surface-unit burner is usually regulated by a separate control valve. This valve opens and closes an internal passageway, allowing more or less gas to flow through the orifice. The amount of gas that flows through the orifice automatically adjusts the air mixture; a smaller amount of gas flow allows a smaller quantity of air to enter the air shutter.

The oven thermostat on many gas ranges operates exactly like the thermostat on most electric ranges. A sensing tube runs from the thermostat into the oven chamber. Inside the tube, a liquid responds to heat changes by expanding or contracting, which in turn opens or closes a switch within the body of the thermostat. The switch controls an electrical coil, called a solenoid, located on the gas line. The solenoid, consisting of coils or wire that are wound around a central armature or plunger, concentrates the magnetic force generated by the electricity flowing through the wires. When the coil is energized, the plunger moves, opening or closing the gas line to the oven burner as required to maintain a specific temperature setting.

Some oven thermostats operate directly on the gas line, moving a bellows arrangement to open or close a disk which, in turn, permits or blocks the flow of gas through the line. Some of these valves modulate — that is, they open or close the gas line gradually rather than instantaneously. A modulating valve reduces any temperature overshooting, and it helps maintain a more constant temperature level.

You can adjust the thermostat of a gas range if the temperature within the oven varies by more than 25 degrees from the setting on the knob. To check the oven temperature, place an accurate thermometer in the center of the oven cavity, and allow the oven burner to stabilize for 30 minutes. If you find a great disparity between the thermometer reading and the knob setting, remove the thermostat knob and look for an adjusting screw. You may find the screw within a hollow thermostat shaft, or you may find it on a movable scale at the rear of the knob skirt. Move the screw or scale until the setting on the knob corresponds with the actual oven temperature.

All gas ovens should have safety devices to shut off the gas flow in case the pilot light goes out. An electrical switch, or a sensing tube, attached to the bellows that controls gas flow within the supply line can do the job. If you have an older range that lacks such a safety feature, contact your local gas company for installation information. This is not a do-

The gas surface unit operates by combining the fuel from the supply line with the correct proportion of air. By the time it reaches the burner, the air/gas mixture is ready to meet the pilot or burner flame.

it-yourself project, however; only an authorized technician should work with the fuel-related components of a gas range.

Many gas ranges feature an electric timer, much like the kind found on many electric ranges. The timer circuit is connected into the circuit of the oven thermostat. When the timer is in its off position, no power goes to the thermostat; the thermostat, therefore, cannot open the valve to allow gas to flow to the oven burner. As you can see, gas ranges do require some electricity, but all you need do is plug the range into a standard 115-volt outlet. Since only the oven valve, timer, and light are electrically powered, a gas range consumes very little current.

Several manufacturers make gas ranges that have a special coating on the inside of the oven liner to provide continuous-cleaning action. This coating contains a catalyst which reacts with food soils and causes them to decompose at normal cooking temperatures. Continuous-cleaning finishes require special consideration, and you must follow the manufacturer's instructions when caring for such ovens. For example, you must never use a commercial oven cleaner on them.

Self-cleaning ovens in gas ranges operate exactly like self-cleaning ovens in electric ranges. The only difference is that the gas burner rather than an electric heating element serves as the heat source.

Gas ranges require little in the way of service. Their electrical components — timer, thermostat, and valve — are subject to failure, but they rarely do fail. Just make sure that the timer is set to a manual or to an operating position when you want to use the oven.

Gas Ranges Troubleshooting Chart

Caution: Unplug the range, turn off the gas supply, and use care in handling when servicing, inspecting or adjusting the range. Replacement parts should only be done by a technician. If you suspect a leak in a gas appliance, turn off gas supply, extinguish all open flames, open windows or doors, and leave the area. Never search for a leak with a match or other open flame. Call an authorized technician or your utility company for a complete inspection before operating the appliance.

PROBLEMS	CAUSES	REPAIRS
Range fails to operate	1. Gas supply shut off.	1. Make sure that the gas is open.
	2. Defective regulator on supply line.	2. Call in an authorized gas technician.
	3. No power to range.	3. Check the electrical receptacle with a table lamp; repair the receptacle if required.
	4. Fuse or circuit breaker in range is open.	4. Check the fuse and replace it if it is open. Reset the circuit breaker.
	5. Pilot flame extinguished.	5. Relight the pilot.
	6. Thermostat defective.	6. Have an authorized technician replace the thermostat.
	7. Timer switch open.	7. Set the timer switch to manual or normal position.
Dirty (sooty) flame	1. Clogged air shutter opening.	1. Check and clean opening.
	2. Air shutter not adjusted properly.	2. Adjust the air shutter to render a good flame.
Surface burners "pop" when turned on	1. Conduction tubes from burner to pilot burner are out of place.	1. Check and place tubes in proper position.
	2. Pilot set too low.	2. Adjust the pilot to proper height (usually about 1/4 of an inch).

Gas burners require cleaning from time to time. Before you perform any sort of service procedure, however, be sure that you shut off the gas supply and unplug the range. You can disassemble many burners, soak them in hot soapy water, and then brush them with an old toothbrush to remove food particles.

If you notice that a burner is starting to clog, you can prevent the clog from worsening by cleaning the blocked orifice with a wooden toothpick. Likewise, if you see that the heat output from a particular burner is reduced below its normal level, use only a soft object (like a toothpick) for cleaning. Since metallic objects can enlarge the orifice openings, they should not be used for cleaning. Should a pilot light become clogged, it might be necessary to unscrew the orifice tip itself and clean the orifice from the inside. The opening in the orifice is generally too small to be cleaned from the outside.

If a burner is hesitant when you turn on the gas supply, check to be sure that the pilot flame is adjusted correctly and that the connecting tubes from the pilot to burner are in place. Again, turn off the gas supply and pull the plug before you attempt any gas range repair. If you smell a gas leak, be sure to call a technician immediately to inspect the range, and do not use the range until it has been examined thoroughly. Open the windows to provide plenty of ventilation, and extinguish any open flames. Natural gas itself has no odor, but the gas company adds an artificial odor to help you detect leaks in gas lines. A leak indicates a situation that is potentially very hazardous. Should you ever smell raw gas in your home, call in professional service personnel immediately.

REFRIGERATORS, FREEZERS, AND AUTOMATIC ICE MAKERS

Refrigerators are relatively simple appliances, and as such they generally provide a long service life. Seldom do they require either major repairs or extensive maintenance. One standard procedure, however, is quite important: You must keep the working components of your refrigerator clean. Remove the dust and dirt that collects around and beneath the appliance frequently. A household vacuum cleaner makes such maintenance a simple task. Be sure to vacuum the condensor coils; it is essential that no unintended "insulation" comes between the refrigerant and the surrounding air.

A refrigerant is a substance that can remove heat. There really is no such thing as "added cold"; cold is, by definition, the absence of heat — just as the color black is not really a color but rather the absence of light. A refrigerant cools by circulating through an enclosed area and absorbing the area's heat. When the heat-laden refrigerant leaves the enclosure, it carries off that which had made the area warm. As a result, the temperature inside the enclosure goes down.

The refrigerant is able to accomplish this task because of a simple law of physics. That is, when a substance evaporates or boils — meaning, when it changes from a liquid to a vapor — it absorbs heat from its surroundings. For example, as water approaches its boiling temperature on a hot stove, it absorbs heat until at 212 degrees F. the water is transformed into steam. Since water has such a relatively high boiling point, though, it is an impractical refrigerant. What is needed for food refrigeration is a substance that evaporates at a much lower temperature.

All refrigeration appliances operate in much the same manner. To provide the cooling effect, the refrigerant circulates through the system. The most commonly used refrigerants have a low boiling point at atmospheric pressure (minus 21 degrees Fahrenheit for R-12; minus 42 degrees for R-22). The low boiling point means that these refrigerants can change from liquid to gaseous states and vice/versa at relatively low pressures and temperatures.

The idea behind all refrigeration appliances is to keep the heat-removing substance in a liquid state until it gets to where the cooling — or heat absorption — is to take place. Then the refrigerant is allowed to vaporize, pulling heat from the surrounding air as it does so. The vaporized cooling substance is carried out of the sealed chamber, reduced to a liquid once again, and the heat is discharged outside the refrigerator.

The entire refrigeration system is a closed loop of copper and steel tubing filled with refrigerant. The compressor is nothing more than a pump to circulate the refrigerant through the loop. In a typical cycle, the compressor pumps the vaporized refrigerant to the condensor, which is the coil of tubing located under (or on the back of) the cabinet. At the condensor outlet is a capillary tube, a tiny piece of copper tubing which acts as an orifice and creates a pressure differential within the system. In the condensor, the refrigerant cools enough to condense into a liquid. It enters the capillary tube as a liquid, but when it goes into the low-pressure area of the evaporator, the refrigerant immediately begins to vaporize and absorb heat. This heat-laden vapor goes back to the compressor, and the cycle is repeated once again.

Evaporation is the liquid-to-vapor cycle, during which the refrigerant absorbs heat and thereby cools the surrounding area. Since the refrigerant vaporizes at a very low temperature, there is no problem in the evaporation stage. The difficulty comes in returning the refrigerant to a liquid so that it can be sent into the sealed cabinet again to vaporize and absorb more heat.

It would be impractical, of course, to try to reduce the refrigerant below its already extremely low boiling point. Fortunately, another law of physics saves the day. If enough pressure is exerted on the refrigerant, it will change back from a vapor to a liquid even though the surrounding temperature is

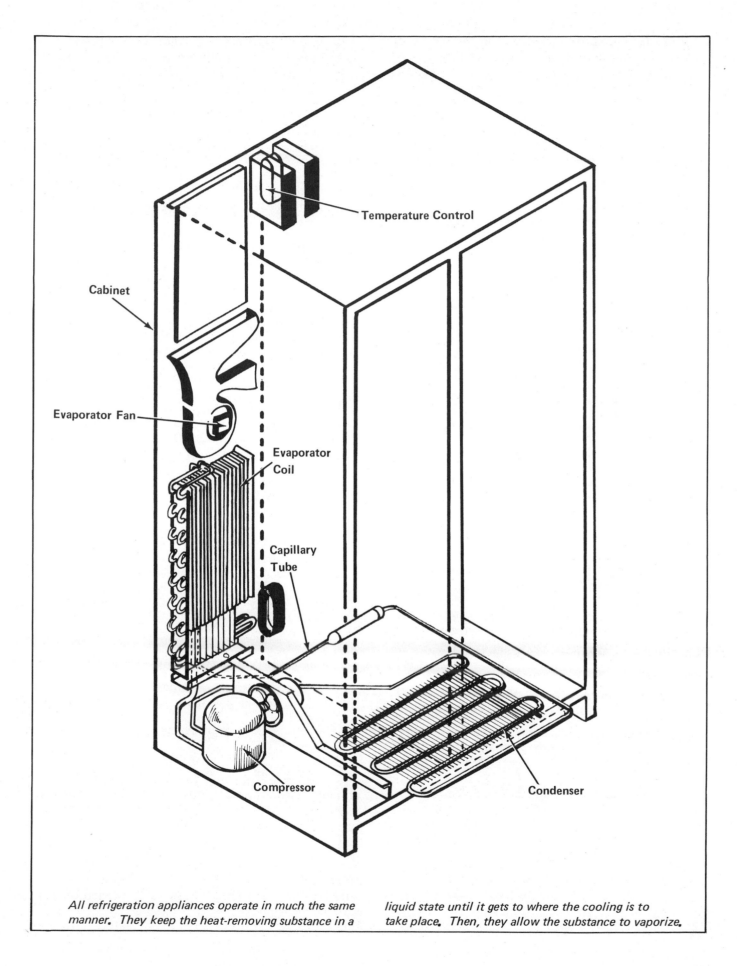

Temperature Control

Cabinet

Evaporator Fan

Evaporator Coil

Capillary Tube

Compressor

Condenser

All refrigeration appliances operate in much the same manner. They keep the heat-removing substance in a liquid state until it gets to where the cooling is to take place. Then, they allow the substance to vaporize.

considerably higher than its boiling point.

The compressor is the segment of the cooling system designed to squeeze the refrigerant back into liquid form. After the refrigerant emerges from the evaporation cycle, it is sent to the compressor. Then, it is moved to the condensor where the heat absorbed during evaporation is discharged outside the refrigerator. The combination of the increased pressure (compressor stage) and the lower temperature (condensor stage) turns the vaporized refrigerant to liquid refrigerant, setting the stage for another evaporation cycle.

When the refrigerant moves from the condensor to the evaporator, it finds tubing of a much greater diameter. The larger tubing means less pressure, and with less pressure, of course, the boiling point drops. The result is that the refrigerant begins to absorb heat and to vaporize. This cycle is continuous — vapor to liquid, liquid to vapor — absorbing heat, discharging the heat outside the refrigerator, and recycling to vaporize and absorb more heat.

If the evaporation cycle were permitted to go on without interruption, the temperature inside the refrigerator would go all the way down to the boiling point of the refrigerant. Therefore, all refrigerators include a thermostat to turn the compressor on and off in response to the temperature levels inside the refrigerator. When the unit is cold enough,

the thermostat shuts down the compressor. As a result, the refrigerant cannot change from a vapor to a liquid, thereby halting the cooling cycle.

The thermostat consists of a long tube filled with a gas or liquid (often the same refrigerant as that used in the cooling system). This sensing tube is sealed at one end, and it has a bellows attached to the opposite end. The tube's contents expand and contract with variations in the temperature surrounding it, causing the bellows to do likewise. This movement, in turn, actuates a switch which turns the compressor on and off to maintain the correct temperature.

Most refrigerators, and many freezers, sold today are called frost-free. Actually, frost develops in these refrigerators and freezers just as it does in all others; but in frostless models, a clock-timer energizes a high-wattage electric heater to defrost the evaporator coil. This defrosting action — done on a regular basis (usually every twelve hours — takes a total of about twenty minutes. Some frostless refrigerators rather than use electric heaters, have an electrically operated valve which allows hot gas to flow into the evaporator coil from the condenser when the timer initiates the defrost cycle.

Most self-defrosting refrigerators have a drain pan located underneath to catch condensate (defrost) water from the evaporator. You should clean this pan at least once every six months to eliminate

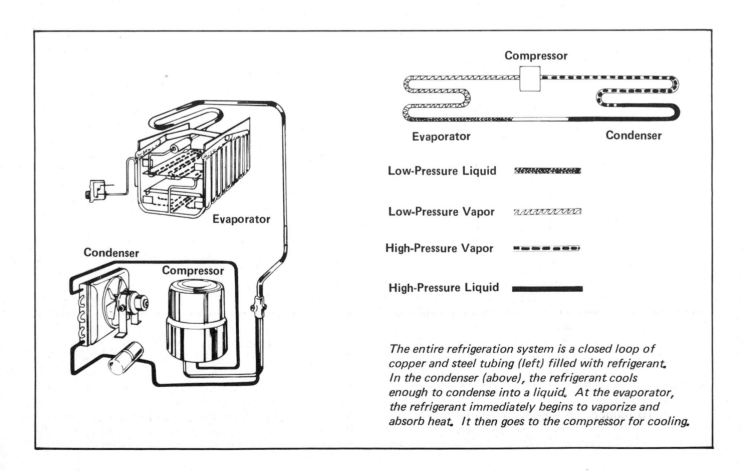

Compressor

Evaporator   Condenser

Low-Pressure Liquid

Low-Pressure Vapor

High-Pressure Vapor

High-Pressure Liquid

Evaporator

Condenser   Compressor

The entire refrigeration system is a closed loop of copper and steel tubing (left) filled with refrigerant. In the condenser (above), the refrigerant cools enough to condense into a liquid. At the evaporator, the refrigerant immediately begins to vaporize and absorb heat. It then goes to the compressor for cooling.

the foul odors from the decayed food particles which drip down with the defrost water. Manual-defrost refrigerators must be defrosted at least twice a year, but you should defrost as soon as the frost thickness approaches one-quarter of an inch. Otherwise, the frost begins to act like an insulation , forcing the refrigerator to consume extra energy.

An automatic ice maker is merely a mold to which a temperature-sensing switch is attached. When the water in the mold reaches a preset temperature (usually around 15 degrees), a motor is energized and the ejection cycle is initiated. As the ice leaves the mold, fresh water flows in to fill it again. A switch senses when the storage bin is full, and it stops the ice-making action at the appropriate time.

If your automatic ice maker suddenly stops working, look for a blockage in the water-inlet valve strainer. To clean these strainers, you must unplug the refrigerator and remove the water line where it enters the valve (usually at the bottom edge of the refrigerator). Then, remove the stainless steel strainer and clean it thoroughly with an old toothbrush.

You can usually trace unpleasant tastes or odors in the ice to uncovered foods in the refrigerator compartment. The odors get picked up and circulated throughout the cabinet, and the ice absorbs them readily. Brown paper bags used for food storage are often responsible for the tastes or odors since these bags have a high sulfur content.

Be sure to unplug your refrigerator before attempting to service it, and take special care to avoid damaging any of the refrigerant-carrying tubing. Few refrigerator problems originate in the sealed system itself. When they do, call in a refrigeration technician. The refrigerants are non-toxic under normal conditions of slight concentration, but they must be handled with care. If you suspect a leak in a refrigerator, open several windows, provide plenty of ventilation, and shut off any open flames (such as pilot lights).

Most refrigeration appliances have a starting relay which starts the compressor motor, and many also have a starting capacitor. Both must be discharged before they can be handled or tested. Since the starting relay or starting capacitor can cause a dangerous or even fatal shock even when the appliance is unplugged, repairing such parts is best left to a professional technician.

Many refrigerators have forced-air condensors; that means they have a small fan to pull air across the warm condensor coils. These condensers must be cleaned regularly, usually every thirty days. Regular cleaning is essential to prevent a lint buildup far back in the condenser coils where you cannot reach it with a vacuum. If you can reach the coils, vacuum them thoroughly with a soft brush attached to the vacuum hose.

To reduce the energy consumption of your refrigerator, position it as far away from any warm air ducts or the range as possible. Test your refrig-

erator's temperature periodically. Put a glass of water in the refrigerator compartment for 24 hours, and then insert a reasonably accurate thermometer in the water. To check the freezer temperature, place the thermometer between several packages of food that have been in the freezer compartment for at least 24 hours. The ideal refrigerator temperature is around 37 degrees, while the temperature in the freezer section should be about zero. A colder refrigerator or freezer does not preserve food any longer, and it costs you more for its higher energy consumption.

Be sure that your refrigerator or freezer is connected to a separate 15-ampere circuit with a grounded outlet. The appliance should have adequate air space above, behind, and on the sides, and never add more warm food than can fit into 10 percent of the unit's storage compartment. The box must be sealed effectively to prevent the hot air outside from entering and warming the closed compartment. Test the seal by closing the refrigerator door on a dollar bill. Next, pull the bill out. If there is no resistance as you pull, the door needs adjusting. The most frequent cause of too much hot air entering the refrigerator, however, is not a failure in the door's sealing ability; it is in the fact that the door is opened too frequently. Make sure that your refrigerator door is opened only as often and for as long as is absolutely necessary to take out or put back the items you refrigerate.

If the compressor runs continuously or excessively, there may be any of several possible problems. You may have the thermostat set too high or the door may not be providing the proper seal. The required repairs are obvious. Other possible causes for the compressor functioning excessively are not so simple to fix. For example, there may be a leak in the system. The thermostat would continually tell the compressor to function, but the unit would not get any cooler because there would be no refrigerant to vaporize in the evaporator coils. You would have to call in a repairman to fix the leak and to recharge the refrigerant.

If, on the other hand, the compressor does not function at all, check for blown fuses or tripped circuit breakers before examining the components of the cooling system. Other possible causes of compressor malfunctions are defective thermostat, defective timer, defective relay, and defective compressor.

If the refrigerator is excessively noisy, you should be able to correct the problem easily. A refrigerator that is not level will clatter; check it with a carpenter's level and adjust the refrigerator's position if so indicated. Of course, a compressor that is loose in its mountings will rattle noisily; merely tighten the mountings to quiet the unit. Finally, the noise may be caused by the tubing of the cooling system hitting against the cabinet of the refrigerator. If this is the case, you should be able to adjust the tubing to prevent it from striking the cabinet.

Refrigerators Troubleshooting Chart

Caution: Unplug appliance before inspecting or repairing. Do not reconnect power until job is completed or while any wiring connections are exposed.

PROBLEMS	CAUSES	REPAIRS
Food storage compartment is too warm	1. Door is opened too often.	1. Open the door only when absolutely necessary.
	2. Thermostat is set at too high a temperature.	2. Readjust thermostat to a lower temperature setting.
	3. Door does not seal tightly.	3. Test the seal by closing the door on a dollar bill. If there is no resistance when you pull on the bill, the door needs adjusting.
	4. Light bulb stays on after door is closed.	4. Test by depressing light bulb button near door. If bulb does not go out, replace defective switch.
	5. Defective defrost system on a frostless refrigerator.	5. Test the defrosting components and replace them if they are faulty.
Compressor runs excessively or never stops running	1. Thermostat is set at too high a temperature.	1. Readjust thermostat to a lower temperature.
	2. Door does not seal tightly.	2. Test the seal by closing the door on a dollar bill. If there is no resistance when you pull on the bill, the door needs adjusting.
	3. Condenser is coated with dust or dirt, preventing refrigerant from liquifying.	3. Remove dust or dirt from condensor coil with a vacuum cleaner to allow air to circulate and cool vaporized refrigerant.
Compressor does not function	1. Fuse is blown or circuit breaker is tripped.	1. Replace fuse or reset circuit breaker.
	2. Thermostat is defective.	2. Test thermostat for continuity and replace if faulty.
	3. Timer is defective.	3. Test timer and replace if faulty.
	4. Relay is defective.	4. Test relay and replace if faulty.
	5. Compressor is broken.	5. Install new compressor or have old one fixed.
Refrigerator is excessively noisy	1. Unit is not level.	1. Check the refrigerator's position with a carpenter's level, and reposition the unit if required.
	2. Compressor is loose in its mountings.	2. Tighten compressor mountings.
	3. Tubing hits against cabinet.	3. Reposition tubing so that it cannot strike the cabinet.
	4. Clogged condenser.	4. Vacuum away lint and dust.
	5. Condenser fan inoperative.	5. Oil fan, or replace it if necessary.